"Finally, a book that goes past the plan to development of an entrepreneurial attitude! Chad Simmons shows the 'want-to-be's' a solution from activation to celebration. Must reading!"

Dr. Don Laney, Executive Director
Cloud L. Cray Center for Entrepreneurial Services
BENEDICTINE COLLEGE

"The Anonymous Entrepreneur *is designed for the thousands of men and women who desire to become entrepreneurs but are reluctant to take the first step. This book will assist them in making that decision.*"

Professor Fran Jabara, Founder
Center for Entrepreneurship
WICHITA STATE UNIVERSITY

"The Anonymous Entrepreneur *offers a 'route of passage' to all who want more than just a job. It will be the handbook for a growing wave of entrepreneurship that shapes society in the next millenium.*"

Richard Thompson, Corporate Executive
Real Estate Entrepreneur

"The Anonymous Entrepreneur *offers a plan to accomplish your goals. And if you don't have any it will open up your mind to create them. Anyone who uses the plan in this book cannot help but succeed to the limits of their vision.*"

William T. Noon, President
Noonshine, Inc.
Former Anonymous Entrepreneur

D1708399

THE
ANONYMOUS
ENTREPRENEUR ™

12 Steps to Build the Entrepreneurial Attitude

To my good Friend Chuck.

CHAD SIMMONS

Chd Simmons

The Corinth Press

First Edition
Library of Congress Catalog Number 97-095021
ISBN 0-9661923-0-3

Cover & interior design by Linda Brems
Production by Premila Malik Borchardt
Edited by Jane Doyle Guthrie

Printed in the United States by Mennonite Press

Published by
The Corinth Press
4200 Somerset, Suite 245
Prairie Village, KS 66208
www.Entrepreneur-America.com

For CB & Bea

Contents

Acknowledgments

Entrepreneurship is a lifestyle of experience with people of all kinds. Some I've met left an impression powerful enough to affect the messages in this book.

Dr. Warren Molton, spiritual mentor and uncommon friend, helped me discover life without limits.

Professor Fran Jabara, extraordinary entrepreneur, is a gifted presence all should encounter.

Close friends Gary Walker, Bob Bone, Bill Noon, and Charlie Podrebarac helped me believe in my topic and myself by taking me seriously.

CEO advisory board members Jerry Venable, Brian Kaufman, and Tom Woods expanded my perspective—like it or not.

United Country partners Lou Francis, Carl Hopkins, and Don Sprague, as well as other company friends, gave me a racetrack to run on filled with priceless experience. Cheryl, you were divine.

Twenty members of my advance focus group read an awful unedited first draft, yet found nice things to say while saying other things nicely.

Wisdom from personal growth programs revealed, then focused, this professional inventory as a useful tool for entrepreneurs. The thousands of pages deleted were as important as the few that are printed.

The title of an important book, *Friends, Partners, & Lovers,* describes the influence of my lovely wife, Lori, toward creation of *The Anonymous Entrepreneur.* Her opinions on all subjects, laughter, and grace nudged me from thesis to antithesis to synthesis.

Foreword

My task in writing a foreword is to recommend, so it is my privilege and personal pleasure to commend this book to you. I have a number of reasons to feel honored and excited about my assignment. First, during the many years that I have known Chad Simmons, I have watched him *become* the ideas in his book. This book is not merely some description of action like an announcer at a game. This man is a player who learns by risking new choices and matures even from his mistakes, unlike others who learn to reject the risk and court cynicism in their mistakes. Moreover, Chad continues to practice in the field of his career. This keeps his writing current with a quality of present tense and timeliness. At the same time, his ideas are time*less*, so that this book may very well become the bible for those of us who want to be truly autonomous, running our careers from the driver's seat rather than being driven by others.

My second reason for accepting Chad's invitation has to do with the heart of the book. The author says it best: "The distinctive difference between this book and others on the topic of entrepreneurship is the focus on the self, not skill, as the greatest agent of change." This, of course, is where every great mission must begin. When Buddha began his teaching, he was asked if he was a god and he said "no," a prophet and he answered "no," a saint and again his response was "no." "Then, who are you?" they asked, and he answered, "I am awake." Buddha means the *enlightened one,* with the unique connotation of one who is aware, alert, conscious of his world. We must begin changing by first waking up to ourselves and our possibilities. Chad knows all about this for himself and for us.

Finally, I am happy to commend this book to you because it resonates with one of my favorite ideas: MAKE IT NEW! There is so much in this book that is new and fresh in approach and application. Any thoughtful reader will be awakened to self-discovery and personal growth toward true entrepreneurship.

Most forewords end with something like "Read this book!" But I say "Live this book," and we will bond with the best of who we are and are becoming. This is the path of the autonomous, anonymous entrepreneur. Welcome aboard!

Dr. Warren Lane Molton
Psychotherapist and Consultant
Kansas City, Missouri

Preface

I was the president and CEO of a national franchise company and enjoyed a substantial ownership interest. It was my third business and, combined with other real estate investments, formed the basis for my career in entrepreneurship. While doing these things I also wrote a book and gained national recognition as a speaker and expert on the topic of business valuation. I even had a pretty good attitude, so it was hard to accept that I could actually be an anonymous entrepreneur. But I was.

Circumstances I created did not permit me to expand and become the vision I had for myself. As a result, no matter how many opportunities I recognized, how exciting they seemed, or how well I converted them into tangible results, the outcome wasn't as satisfying as expected. I had the right vision but the wrong reality, and I started to wonder if others like me existed and had done the same.

As I began to focus on others who might share my experiences and desires, I discovered I was not alone. Anonymous entrepreneurs were everywhere, and we all had something in common. We frequently started our business ownership with the acquisition of business assets—not the business attitude. It is a common mistake, but the trappings of an entrepreneur do not make entrepreneurship a reality. The entrepreneurial attitude does.

I began to consider my transition to success by reexamining my attitude and working to improve it first. To help I found many books describing what to do to operate a business. There were very few, however, that described the secret ingredient of entrepreneurs—their attitude of success.

In the final analysis I discovered, when things are not going the way we want, how we often (and often incorrectly) begin a journey by questioning "why" circumstances are what they are. "Why's" don't matter though to entrepreneurs; solutions do. The 12 steps that form the core of *The Anonymous Entrepreneur* create a road map for a rewarding journey. They were my solution and I believe they can be yours.

CHAPTER ONE

YOUR TRANSITION BEGINS

An anonymous entrepreneur could be anyone dissatisfied with his or her current career choice. One of two identifying conditions normally exist:

1. *Right vision—wrong reality.* Usually a person who works for someone else, this anonymous entrepreneur has good vision and can see ways to improve existing opportunities or expand into new areas. But without the necessary authority to take action, it's not possible to build on these ideas. Such anonymous entrepreneurs find frustration in the orthodoxies of a business. Their prime directive is finding a way to link their vision to employment circumstances that will allow them to express it. Financial and creative fulfillment are their goals, and business ownership often proves the best vehicle for it.

2. *Wrong vision—right reality.* Fascinating as it might seem, a large percentage of the 22 million entrepreneurs who own small businesses in America are anonymous. Not because their ownership interest is confidential, though—it's because they have the right reality but no vision. Figuratively speaking, they're all dressed up with no place to go. Their businesses may flounder along as a result, always taking two steps forward and one step back.

Either condition just described can lead to becoming an anonymous entrepreneur. Finding a way to reset the relationship between vision and reality is the key to making a transition. When this is done, the all-important derivatives of entrepreneurship (profit, wealth, and freedom of choice) have a fertile venue for growth.

Could you be an anonymous entrepreneur? Do you have ideas but no place to try them? Or do you already own a business but seem frustrated by the daily grind of effort that doesn't seem to go anywhere? Are you plagued by feelings of uncertainty, complacency, and frustration? Answering "yes" to these questions about your career choice (as well as to those in "Am I an Anonymous Entrepreneur?") may help you decide if you, too, are an anonymous entrepreneur.

THE ENTREPRENEURIAL CLASS According to the United States Small Business Administration, nearly 30 percent of Americans are thinking of starting a business at any given time. With a population of approximately 275 million, that's 91 million would-be entrepreneurs hoping for a better way to achieve creative fulfillment and financial autonomy.

Geography, social standing, economic status, gender, race, or sexual or religious orientation do not define anonymous entrepreneurs. They are people of all ages, skills, and personality types, who may work for someone else or for themselves.

Today's more prominent and rapidly growing groups of anonymous entrepreneurs include those who own a small business or want to buy one, franchisees, multilevel marketers, home-based business owners, professionals, telecommuters, people who operate a part-time business in the hopes that one day it will become a full-time occupation, women seeking opportunity, college professors and students, retiring military professionals, dissatisfied corporate executives, and even mature persons coming out of retirement for a shadow career as entrepreneurs.

What do anonymous entrepreneurs have in common? They are uncertain about their professional future and have neither the creative fulfillment nor the financial results they want. Feelings of uncertainty, complacency, and frustration are old friends because these people don't know anything else is possible. This is important to recognize in yourself—otherwise you, too, could be and remain an anonymous entrepreneur.

AM I AN ANONYMOUS ENTREPRENEUR?

1. Do I avoid change but know it must occur?
2. Do I hear my instincts guiding me but fail to listen?
3. Does reliance on one of my strengths ever cause me a problem?
4. Am I secretly waiting for "the opportunity of a lifetime"?
5. When I enter a business, do I see ways to improve it?
6. Do my big ideas seem like silly dreams better off left unspoken?
7. Do I hear others say what I was thinking but lacked the confidence to share?
8. Does it feel good when others look up to me at work?
9. Do I sometimes feel like I'm the only one who sees the "real" problem?
10. Do I think risk and problems are good things?
11. Am I not getting enough money and creative fulfillment from my work?
12. Are high ethics important to me?
13. Have I tried to save money but not been too successful?
14. Do things at work seem to get overcomplicated?
15. If I fail, would I prefer it to be my fault instead of someone else's?
16. Do I agree with the idea of goal setting but never set them myself?
17. Am I often taken by surprise or not ready when I should be?
18. Would I rather be a rule breaker than a rule keeper or follower?
19. Do I fail to celebrate my professional accomplishments?
20. Do I own a business or wish I did?

If you answered "yes" to many of these questions, you may be an anonymous entrepreneur with the foundation to become a successful one. Developing the entrepreneurial attitude might make a big difference.

The idea of matching vision to reality may seem lofty, theoretical, and unimportant, but it has very practical applications. One quality of highly successful entrepreneurs is the ability to match their strengths (visions)—as well as those of the people they hire—with challenging responsibilities (realities). In this way everyone involved can become empowered and grow. Empowered employees are the secret ingredient for business growth because they allow the entrepreneur leader to take advantage of new, often unexpected opportunities.

THE ENTREPRENEURIAL ENVIRONMENT If you were a marketer, you would call anonymous entrepreneurs a marketing opportunity. They have what it takes to succeed in this new information world but haven't made that discovery yet. Helping them do it represents opportunity. You, as an anonymous entrepreneur, hold that opportunity to develop yourself.

In this instant economy, there is no job or opportunity that will last a lifetime. You will not retire from your work in 30 years with a gold watch. Your job will probably be transformed or eliminated within 10 years. If you don't change, your employment will likely be terminated. Management that works to make things cheaper, faster, better is not the key to success today—being different is.

Entrepreneurs express their difference and win by changing the rules of the game. They challenge the sacred cows that continue to exist in business only because someone considers them sacred—not because they deliver any more milk. Entrepreneurs will shake up the place, convert absurdities into profitable realities, and give conventional management a reason to hesitate. That is an entrepreneur's greatest asset—they force everyone to think new.

Entrepreneurs have vision, but very importantly they know how to energize others to adopt that vision.

They can take action and guide others to do the same, producing results. Successful entrepreneurs may start each day with nothing to do but will have one or more activities launched by day's end. Many anonymous entrepreneurs try lots of new ways of doing things and will change landscapes frequently if necessary. This willingness to embrace change is their greatest strength.

Entrepreneurs are natural leaders who attract others.

Today we live in an instantaneous economy. New information spreads at an amazing speed. As a result, businesses must be quick to adapt. Traditional management, long-time protector of the status quo, is quickly becoming a back-room player, still important but not the savior of profit. Entrepreneurs, on the other hand, deliver "what can be," and in this age of rapid change are charging to the forefront.

Your share of wealth in business will more likely come from new wealth created than from an expanding share of what already exists. So it pays not to get too excited about programs you create today, since you may need to blow them up in six months to implement new ones. Such is the state of change in the new world of business, and nobody handles change better than an entrepreneur.

"Web organizations"—an increasing part of the entrepreneurial arena—offer communication linkages in all directions from one source. These have the potential to replace cumbersome production-line companies with top-down or bottom-up management and communication. The best examples of web-type organizations are those created by home-based entrepreneurs. Using outsourcing, a computer, and communication networks, these professionals can provide much of the work previously required by an organization with employees. They can work from home to reduce their overhead, so there's no need for a static organization.

A team of like-minded entrepreneurs who are

linked for long- or short-term projects can communicate with lightning speed and be extremely flexible. This enables them to quickly exploit business opportunities. In addition, using these same resources they can access a global marketplace, reaching in days the same number of customers it used to take years to contact. Their greatest challenge is learning to maintain and energize a team of people who work with them but not for them.

Entrepreneurs are well suited to this new environment, flush with web-type organizations, instant communications, and change. Anonymous entrepreneurs can be, too, if they prepare themselves to make the transition. Unfortunately, too many think this means changing jobs or buying a business. These are often premature solutions. There is another, less costly way that can produce ever greater results for those seeking the transition to successful entrepreneurship. This solution is one practiced by all entrepreneurs and enables them to take on any challenge. They build and maintain The Entrepreneurial Attitude.

THE ENTREPRENEURIAL ATTITUDE The popularity of programs such as TQM (Total Quality Management) and KAIZEN (Constant Improvement) have helped business increase market share, lower costs, and improve profits in years past. But they are product-oriented strategies that focus on "what is" instead of "what is to come"; thus, their focus on existing wealth is a sentence of poor results at best or failure ultimately.

In the fast-paced world of change, there is no place for one's entire focus to rest on existing products because that's not the true source of success. Many of today's major success stories didn't even exist a decade ago. Management is important, to ensure that a new product has a productive life-span, but entrepreneurs are required to spawn new ideas and create new wealth by converting old market share into new. People who can adapt to change and recognize the opportunities it creates are your most valuable resource. The *entrepreneurial attitude* is the distinguishing mark separating successful entrepreneurs from their anonymous counterparts. Without this particular mind-set, the benefits of entrepreneurship—profit, wealth, and choice—are elusive. To deconstruct your old attitude and mismatch of vision and reality (which keeps you anonymous), you must explore the possibility of change from within. Building an entrepreneurial attitude is completely free but has the potential to pay the biggest dividends. It's the best investment value to you.

The feelings evoked by successful entrepreneurship are different from those shared by anonymous entrepreneurs. Successful entrepreneurs have vision to guide them, use tension as a positive force to energize their vision, and take action to validate their effort by producing results. The difference between entrepreneurs who remain anonymous and those who don't isn't skill—it's attitude.

New careers begin like the last one ended.

Think of the entrepreneurial attitude this way. Suppose you're attempting to loosen a rusty bolt. Pulling on the wrench takes all your strength and won't break the bolt free. If you add a short length of pipe to the handle of the wrench, the physics of your effort change. Now when you apply pressure the uncooperative bolt loosens easily. The action of the wrench and the bolt are completely unchanged. But the extension of the handle complements the effort so the job is done quickly and with less effort. This is a changed way to work with existing resources.

Your work is the rusty bolt. Your skill is your wrench. The extension of the handle is your attitude. How big is it? How big do you want it to be?

THE ENTREPRENEURIAL
PROFILE

Businesses may or may not succeed with tried-and-true accounting, marketing, production, administration, or sales efforts. You can readily hire a host of people to do these things. But it's difficult to imagine a business succeeding without an entrepreneurial influence at the top to offer creative insight, recognize what others cannot see, build enthusiasm, and translate ideas into action that gets results. These are essential to create and sustain a business successfully. Where, however, can you hire a person who does all that? Where do you hire entrepreneurs?

Entrepreneurs will work 16 hours a day for themselves to keep from having to work half that for someone else.

Entrepreneurship often begins as a part-time or home-based "do-it-yourself" operation. It takes time and commitment to build an entrepreneurial attitude. It also takes skinning your knees from time to time. Often failure for an entrepreneur is just a pratfall on the path to success. Consider Newton's third law of motion—"for every action there is an equal and opposite reaction." Recognize every downside has an upside of equal or greater proportion. Every problem extends you an opportunity to find a solution someone will buy.

At 28 years of age I committed all my time and resources to making one business deal happen. It brought me a six-figure bonus. Three weeks after closing, the principals changed their minds. I was not so inclined but, in the final analysis, was forced to return my earnings.

I shared this experience with a friend who was a successful jeweler and entrepreneur. My future looked bleak. But my friend surprised me by suggesting I write a book about the techniques I developed to create such transactions in the first place. All my limited vision could see was how much was lost by one deal that fell apart. With his powerful entrepreneurial attitude, my friend could see how much was made in other deals that didn't.

I took this man's advice and wrote *Rule of Thumb:*

The Standard in Pricing Small Businesses. In the years since publication, that book has led me to more employment, investment, and speaking opportunities than I could ever have imagined. Problems create opportunities for those willing to see them.

No failure or obstacle is so big that it should keep you from your vision of success. Tomorrow is a new beginning and it always comes. The fact that you are reading this book says enough about how much you care to discover a new attitude and thereby your own unlimited potential.

CHAPTER TWO

SCALING THE GROWTH WALL

Finding the right match between vision and reality is one way to launch yourself out of anonymity. But it isn't enough to ensure continued forward motion. The edge on your entrepreneurial attitude that led to success through change must be maintained. This is especially hard to do when business is favorable and things are going well—these can be seductive times. Because if you think the world is standing still around you, think again. Someone is already planning ways to convert your success into their next opportunity. In a challenging environment such as business people face today, the rules of engagement change with speed and frequency. You must do the same; when you don't, a growth wall will spring up.

A growth wall is a condition that prevents progress and results. It stops you dead in your tracks. The concept of a growth wall is especially important to understand in times of great change because anonymous entrepreneurs run into them when the changes in their business environment have continued but they have not kept pace. As a result their vision gradually falls farther and farther behind the marketplace reality.

**"We are two years away from failure."
BILL GATES
Microsoft, Inc.**

When a growth wall occurs, you develop uncertainty about the future, complacency toward your opportunity, and frustration about your progress. Left unchecked, it can grow more pronounced and smother a business or career. Growth walls have the power to bring down any business, regardless of size.

The concept of a growth wall in business is not new. Richard Osborne, a professor at Case Western Reserve University, described a Phase Two Entrepreneurial Growth Wall as common in the evolution of owner-managed entrepreneurial companies. He noted several patterns inherent in companies that failed to penetrate a growth wall, including 1) sudden reversals in

KNOW THE SIGNS

revenue after steady annual business increases; 2) diminished entrepreneurial energy; 3) generalized internal focus; 4) falling behind the industry trend change curve; 5) reactive product development, distribution, and marketing; and 6) absence of internal attitudes and competencies necessary to see and understand external threats.

To break through a growth wall, company managers must reestablish the link between their product and their market—the latter has changed while the former has not. For example, being a superb manufacturer of bell-bottomed jeans has little value when there's no demand. So, to prevent growth walls, business owners should continuously observe the environment in which they operate and stimulate complementary changes within their businesses as needed.

We tend to assume people with the longest company association will know best how to prevent or penetrate a growth wall. Unfortunately, experience creates a disadvantage. Thomas E. Woods, former Chief Financial Officer of TransWorld Airlines, shared this wise insight with me: "We ran our company efficiently and we did it well. We experienced the typical challenges of running a large business, meeting them all directly and aggressively. Eventually, our management team became so experienced at anticipating problems we knew which solutions proposed by younger executives would or would not work. As a consequence, many were quickly rejected and never tried. Eventually I realized we had become so smart that we had become the problem."

A growth wall had worked itself into the ranks of senior management of this multinational company. They had all the answers for a marketplace environment that existed in the past—but not the present.

If a growth wall can work itself into the ranks of a company filled with high-powered business talent, it certainly can creep into a business with less intellectual capital. As conditions change constantly, yesterday's unwanted solutions might become valuable answers for today's problems. Talk to friends and advisors outside your loop to sound out your problems—new blood and fresh eyes can often see the value of different approaches. By keeping an open mind the small business person (particularly a home-based entrepreneur) can use change as a competitive opportunity. Big companies have money but not speed and adaptability.

When you are first to the market with a new idea, everyone else is not.

Staying at the forefront of what's new keeps you sharp and penetrates your entrepreneurial attitude, which ultimately turns out business tactics tuned to marketplace realities. This prevents growth walls from limiting the benefits you seek through entrepreneurship.

DON'T GET BACK TO BASICS

A common reaction to poor business performance is the mandate to "get back to basics." Translated, that means do what you did when business was doing well. This feels like a safe approach but instead often signals a leader with a closed mind unwilling to learn and change. If you want to expose this perspective, ask key people how long it's been since they attended a self-improvement program or read a book along those lines. If it's been more than a year, that tells you something.

Growth walls find their openings when original solutions turn unproductive. The market has moved forward, extinguishing demand for the original product or service. Does it make sense to keep producing them? Getting back to basics is, many times, not the best solution for a growth wall—the basics *are* the problem.

When management stays in touch with the marketplace, up-to-date information can consistently shape the productivity of existing resources. Your products and services thus don't become prematurely outdated.

Operational change like this takes courage because it means leaving the original success story in the past. But, relax, another one waits around the next corner.

MY GROWTH WALL

Many good people have been wasted on a good job.

I was a successful commercial real estate and business broker with my own franchised practice. While visiting my favorite client in California, word came of an offer to become national sales manager for the company I had been affiliated with previously. It sounded like an attractive growth opportunity.

The assignment I accepted had the makings of a growth wall from the first day. In my enthusiasm to move up, I failed to compare the values of my co-executives with my own. They were very different. This became clear years later when, after we acquired the company, one partner confided in me that in becoming an owner he had already achieved more than he ever expected. I, on the other hand, was just beginning to run. My associates were not motivated to go where I was heading. Nevertheless, I went on to become the president and CEO of the company with the intent to provide entrepreneurial values in leadership consistent with the challenges ahead. But the foundation of my original growth wall was still in place.

The management team had never built the entrepreneurial attitude needed to penetrate the company's growth wall. Uncertainty was high and we dangled at the mercy of the market. Complacency encroached on staff morale, and frustration had become a way of life. My first act in the leadership role was to focus on external tactics—changing *what* we did instead of *how* we did things. It was a quick fix and not a substitute for a long-term solution.

Next, to overcome growth walls looming over my company, my management team, and myself, I felt it was important to separate the benefits of ownership from the benefits of employment. This was important because my partners and I were owners *and* operating management. To grow it seemed we needed a mentality that would expand our vision and ideas, generate excitement about making them happen, and encourage productivity to improve performance. With the help of a blue-ribbon CEO Advisory Board serving double-duty as a compensation committee, I developed three adjustments which were recommended for consideration of my partners. These involved 1) a performance-based compensation plan, 2) authority to encourage accountability centralized in one leader instead of a committee, and 3) increased accountability of this leader (for results) to the Board of Directors.

The rejection of all three adjustments that followed was a de facto rejection of my entrepreneurial and leadership values. I resigned and, to my surprise, immediately knocked down my growth wall.

You have to get out of your comfort zone if you want to grow. Imagine that the box below is everything you are—all your beliefs and values. Anything outside the box is what you're not.   **CAST A WIDER NET**

YOU

Each time you learn something new, notice what happens:

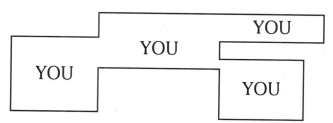

Little by little you start to get bigger. When you continue to learn new information and change, you grow. But if you stop, you start looking like this:

$$\boxed{\text{YOU}}$$

Change is a constant in our lives. If you're not moving forward to create a better entrepreneurial attitude, you're not keeping up with your needs. In fact you're moving backward—and shrinking by comparison with others who continue to grow. Change is necessary to sustain a productive environment filled with the recognition and excitement of new opportunities exploited for their profit potential. Only through such transition can you prevent your career objectives from fading over time. If they go soft, so does your entrepreneurial attitude, and with it your performance.

Generally the burden of allowing a growth wall to stay in place is greater than whatever it takes to remove it. A leap into entrepreneurial oblivion could not be worse than rotting away with uncertainty, complacency, and frustration. My worst day now is better than my best day back then.

But my change was a hard transition to make. Where the phone once rang endlessly, now there were no calls. A daily agenda that was once too full was now an empty slate. Nobody looked up to or down at me. I became temporarily invisible, and my corporate ego evaporated. Was it a mistake? No. It was the smartest move I ever made. I got my entrepreneurial attitude back and set my feet on the path of different behaviors. That's the key to producing different results. And I have.

THE VALUE OF UNIQUENESS Do all anonymous entrepreneurs experience the growth wall phenomenon? Probably, at one time or another. Most successful entrepreneurs have stared failure in the eye, even though they may not talk about it much. Such experiences can prove a most valuable resource, however, because of the education they offer. The solutions they impart can keep you from stacking the bricks for new and bigger growth walls in the future. Such invigorating challenges help maintain a performance-oriented entrepreneurial attitude and the personal fulfillment that follows. The more skillfully you match the benefits of your work to your needs for fulfillment, the greater the chances are that you can succeed.

Recognizing and fostering uniqueness, therefore, becomes a form of business insurance. Knowing what is unique about yourself and/or your company offers a smart way to prevent the anonymous entrepreneur's growth wall. Each of us embodies a one-of-a-kind combination of experience, behaviors, skills, and action. The deeper you dig to discover who you are, the better your chance of integrating those distinctive aspects into your work or business. That creates a marketing differentiation—sets your business apart from all others as clearly as your own individuality. Doing so has the potential to improve financial results. In the process you realize greater fulfillment from your work since it's a clearer expression of you.

Most successful business people, especially entrepreneurs, derive the greatest satisfaction from their work when it involves creative activity. Effort of this kind is exciting and leads to superior performance. It's easy to recognize entrepreneurs who have found their niche—they often can't believe they're paid to do what they do. This is what you and I are looking for and what the entrepreneurial attitude can help us find. Money is just a natural by-product of this mind-set. Growth walls aren't.

Entrepreneurs and other small business owners burn out when the business doesn't keep pace with their needs. Passing through the wall means changing to accommodate the present, not the past. Start by breaking up the routine. Perhaps take a vacation and preserve a career, or hire someone else to run the business. If the latter proves successful, it's the highest accomplishment of an entrepreneur—it shows the business has taken on a life of its own.

The shifts and transitions required to do all this takes courage, but that's usually in ample supply when you move in the direction of individuality. This vital market differentiation gives your business its best shot at staying bulletproof. And wallproof.

CHAPTER THREE

"MBA"–MANAGEMENT BY ATTITUDE

To create a mental image of the entrepreneurial attitude, you can compare it to the attitude of an aircraft. The pilot adjusts the wing surfaces before takeoff to provide the lift needed to fly. These adjustments create the plane's best attitude for flight in existing conditions. Without the right attitude, no amount of speed, fuel, runway distance, or pilot skill will get the plane off the ground.

Extending the metaphor, it takes more than education and graduate degrees to leave the tarmac of anonymity. Despite the value of advanced learning and the discipline required to achieve it, there's something else that contributes significantly to business success and can be learned by those without the time or money for higher education: the Entrepreneurial Attitude.

College MBA curricula often include a focus on advanced accounting, business law, marketing, and finance. But entrepreneurs seldom fail due to a lack of expertise in these disciplines—if you need such resources, you can find others to provide them. Failure occurs more often because, like an aircraft, someone doesn't have the right attitude. Skills gained from an MBA program should be complemented with an entrepreneur's MBA—Management by Attitude—to achieve maximum results.

Proven entrepreneurs rise in the ranks of success because they have the right attitude. In fact, the absence of a properly positioned attitude may be all that stands between dreams and reality for many anonymous entrepreneurs. Developing and maintaining it has little to do with skill and much to do with self-discovery of weaknesses and strengths. You may not recognize the need to adjust your surfaces, or behaviors, to create an attitude for flight. Or you may not know how to do it. The Entrepreneur's 12-Step Program can offer a revealing guide to financial autonomy.

A BLUEPRINT FOR
ATTITUDE A paradigm is an example or illustration that serves as a framework for understanding. We can use a paradigm, or diagram, to explain the attitude of entrepreneurs. This diagram has three parts, which include objective, positive, and negative aspects of attitude that serve to describe how we believe, think, feel, act, and guide ourselves to success.

The diagram below derives from a concept of unity developed by Dr. Warren Lane Molton, a psychotherapist and business consultant who authored the book *Friends, Partners, & Lovers*:

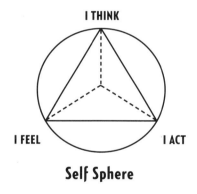

Self Sphere

In Dr. Molton's view, autonomy depends greatly on one's understanding of self as a thinking, feeling, acting, and believing person. *Believing,* he says, relates to the values, philosophy, or theology that gives us understanding of life's meaning. *Thinking,* by contrast, invites reasoning, comprehending, judging, and remembering, which draw on goal-centered ideas, symbols, metaphors, and associations as stimulated by a need or task and leading toward a realistic solution. *Feeling,* in Dr. Molton's model, describes the "color of life," including all the hues, tones, tints, and intensity of one's full emotional spectrum. *Acting*, finally, comprises energy or movement, the "doing" and causing things to occur for change, growth, and development.

The center of the diagram, in Dr. Molton's words, "directs, instructs, and equips the business of the other three areas." Thinking, feeling and acting are the positive behavioral aspects we use to work. When fully connected, things come easier for the would-be entrepreneur. When one aspect is deficient or not present at all, this creates an unpleasant experience, identified on the diagram opposite the missing aspect of attitude.

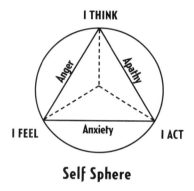

Self Sphere

More importantly, when one positive aspect of your attitude is missing, the total system is short-circuited and you must operate with the other two. For example, if you don't think about how you run your business, you're left to operate on feelings and action. This means running a business without a business plan—not a good idea. Worse, you'll constantly feel plagued with anxiety because of uncertainty about where you're heading. Some call this crisis management. You can see how this applies to feeling and acting, too, when they're out of the picture. Remove the former and apathy appears; the latter and you experience anger.

THE ENTREPRENEUR'S ATTITUDE DIAGRAM Warren Molton's paradigm, or model, can describe people, businesses, or relationships. An entrepreneurial attitude diagram is one such application to anonymous entrepreneurs. It illustrates the links between forces that favorably influence an entrepreneurial attitude and those that do not. When the linkage is complete, successful results will likely occur. Understanding this diagram clearly will make it easier to identify your own strengths and weaknesses, and then improve.

An anonymous entrepreneur's objective is ultimately to have his or her own business. However, to proceed in the most fruitful sequence, one should set that aside in favor of another goal that's more practical and valuable: establish the entrepreneurial attitude first, and it facilitates achieving the previous objective.

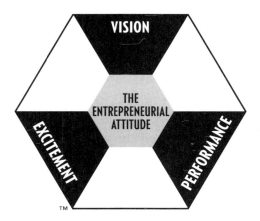

A positive aspect of the entrepreneurial attitude that anonymous entrepreneurs must be able to recognize is a *vision* of opportunity *(think)* when they see it. This crucial step begins with your first idea for a new business venture and all those related to it that follow.

After defining a vision, anonymous entrepreneurs must articulate it to themselves and others. If it's a vision consistent with a marketplace reality, it will create a sense of *excitement.* This is so important because no entrepreneur succeeds alone. Others must be motivated before they can offer their help and important support.

Finally, anonymous entrepreneurs need to develop a *performance (acting)* orientation. Ray Kroc, the founder of McDonald's, once said, "There are thousands of people with exciting ideas but only a few who will do anything about them." You may have observed that many people use so much thinking and emotional energy to talk about what they want to do, there isn't any left to take action. The energy used to talk about ideas is better spent doing something about them.

Think first. Feel second. Act third. Then let your results do your talking for you.

In the entrepreneurial attitude diagram, vision, excitement, and performance connect to form a complete system. When one element isn't present, the system has to operate without it. Worse, a negative aspect takes its place: uncertainty, complacency, or frustration.

Negative Aspects of the Diagram

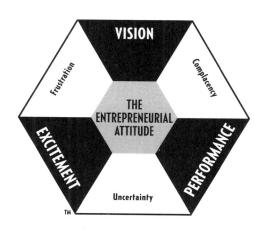

As long as you can recognize opportunities and goals, the direction you're heading will be clear. When your vision is cloudy, though, you become anxious about the future and *uncertainty* grows. To work using only excitement and performance is the equivalent of shooting in the dark—hitting any target is based on luck. You can't rely on success as function of luck alone.

Failing to develop a sense of excitement about your work will leave you staring at the glass ceiling or contemplating the orthodoxy of management unwilling to change—an invitation to *complacency* (apathy). In this mental state you just don't care about the work anymore. Would you want employees working for you who don't care about their work or your business? How successful can you be then if *you* don't care?

Real *frustration* grows in the absence of performance. You may have worked with people in positions of authority who talked a good game but did little to speak of. They usually attach themselves to small issues, steering clear of bigger problems until they're forced to handle them. They often promise performance again and again but never produce. You can imagine why the frustration level gets pretty high.

I once terminated the employment of a division vice president even though he was one of my favorite people. The entrepreneurial attitude that made him so effective was gone. He still had his ability to recognize opportunity, but his excitement for the job was missing. In addition, his performance had become completely inadequate as he just "went through the moves." I don't think I hurt him by terminating his employment as much as I helped him. Leaving a company after 30 years really woke him up. His entrepreneurial attitude was reignited and he became vital again.

Successful entrepreneurs have taught themselves to recognize opportunity, create excitement, and perform to get results. Doing these things successfully also inspires others to follow. Find ways to keep your business simple, to manage risk, to make ideas attractive, and to work according to a plan. Entrepreneurs functioning this way are often characterized as intelligent, courageous, attractive, methodical, and forward thinking. Anonymous entrepreneurs have many of the same qualities lying dormant—wake them up.

Let's return to our airplane comparison. Recall the **DEVELOPING LIFT** right attitude creates the lift needed to fly. Likewise, changes in the attitude of the anonymous entrepreneur make it easier for him or her to deliver results. The more powerful the attitude, the better the results created. Can this be measured? An entrepreneur's quotient or "EQ" provides a convenient way to do so while keeping the focus on maintaining a healthy entrepreneurial attitude.

By putting forth the effort to build a stronger, more fully functioning entrepreneurial attitude, EQ rises. Successful entrepreneurs obviously have a high EQ— they function at peak levels. They also surround themselves with people who have high EQs because they're not intimidated by them. In fact, they're eager to hire people smarter and more capable than themselves. Skill does not make an entrepreneur—attitude does.

When the sum of combined actions is greater than the individual effects, synergy is created. Synergy between recognition, excitement, and performance has the potential to deliver exponential results. Think of it as similar to compounding with money. Interest earns more interest as well as the principal it came from in the first place. Behaviors that support entrepreneurship foster the evolution of more behaviors that do more of the same. Ideas, excitement, and performance can become self-sustaining.

An old friend of mine is an architect who worked

for 10 years without significant financial success. He married a woman with terrific entrepreneurial attitude and he caught it from her. His exceptional skills, complemented by this new attitude, changed his circumstances dramatically. He landed the best projects, relocated to a stylish office, added staff, invested in real estate, and built a beautiful home. Then they sold everything and retired. They bought a huge motorhome and traveled the country, but eventually he came out of retirement to become the lead architect for a worldwide company. He was always a good architect; he became a successful one when, with some inspiration from his wife, his entrepreneurial attitude emerged.

What is the level of your entrepreneurial quotient? A self-evaluation follows on the next page. You can complete it for yourself plus have someone else do one about you for comparison purposes. Review areas where improvement might be needed and consider them opportunities to raise your EQ.

LINKAGE TO ESCAPE VELOCITY Different tactics produce different results. After 10 years in the corporate environment, I had the chance to use my talents for myself instead of everyone else. Changing my reality to match my vision felt like a big weight was lifted from my shoulders. I got excited.

Performance, after my departure from the corporate world, was not as difficult as I expected. I had lots of time to focus on me and my priorities. Within six months I had completed a surprising amount of personal projects that had been on hold for years. Plus, I sold some impressive real estate, drafted a new edition of my business valuation book, and collected my ideas about entrepreneurship in *The Anonymous Entrepreneur*. The objective of this book is to help you discover how to remove limitations on your own success. Then you are free to imagine and explore the possibilities of you.

THE ENTREPRENEURIAL QUOTIENT "EQ" TEST

Using a colored pencil, place a dot on the line between each pair of words closest to the one that best describes you. When complete, connect the dots with a line. Examine your results, noticing that marks to the right of the midline are the qualities of an entrepreneur.

RELAXED	COMPETITIVE
FINANCIALLY SATISFIED	WANTS MORE $$$'S
PREFERS ORGANIZATION	COMFORTABLE WITH CHAOS
RESERVED	WILLING
COMFORTABLE	RESTLESS
LIKES PROTOCOL	CREATIVE
APATHETIC	OPTIMISTIC
INSECURE	SELF-CONFIDENT
PASSIVE	AGGRESSIVE
PROMOTIONAL	ATTRACTIVE
ACCEPTS STANDARDS	SETS STANDARDS
PREFERS TEAMWORK	CAN WORK ALONE
FOLLOWER	SELF-STARTER
AVOIDS RESPONSIBILITY	LIKES ACCOUNTABILITY
TIRES EASILY	ENERGETIC
9:00 TO 5:00	24-HOUR CLOCK
DOES NOT GO TO SEMINARS	LIKES TO LEARN
NOT GOAL ORIENTED	SETS WRITTEN GOALS
DOESN'T MANAGE TIME	TIME MANAGER
QUIET	COMMUNICATIVE
RISK IS BAD	RISK IS GOOD
ROUTINE ORIENTED	PROBLEM SOLVER

"Successful behaviors create success."

Since getting started and staying on track are the hardest part of any transition or self-improvement plan, these success behaviors need to be prioritized, individualized, and then internalized. In the Entrepreneur's 12-Step Program that follows in Chapter Four, a compilation of effective information is integrated within a practical process, a proven way to create powerful results. An anonymous entrepreneur is a person who can create a better job by filling holes in his or her career with blocks of good attitude. Without even realizing it, successful entrepreneurs do this all the time.

THE ENTREPRENEUR'S 12-STEP PROGRAM

An American industrialist asked a famous Japanese artist to create a painting for his new home. The completed canvas was quite large. In the center stood a small cherry tree bearing a few blossoms and one bird perched on a lower branch. There was nothing else. The industrialist asked, "Why did you leave all this space empty?" The artist replied, "To give the bird a place to fly."

Your transition to entrepreneurship is also a sort of canvas. As an anonymous entrepreneur, your first picture attempts may be cluttered with extraneous elements that do not serve you or your journey to entrepreneurship. Some may need to be removed to make room for your entrepreneurial flight. The Entrepreneur's 12-Step Program offers a comprehensive selection of paints and brushes with which to compose an authentic representation of your dreams and business vision.

AN ECONOMICAL METHOD

The problem with most self-improvement programs is they take too much effort to get results. Or they are very costly. This diversion of resources and attention can make it difficult to realize the intended benefits. Sometimes we're lucky to retrieve the original investment of energy, money, and time. Ideally a self-improvement program should expand on existing resources and offer an unlimited potential for growth.

Proponents of self-improvement programs often say, "You get out of the program what you put into it." That's not enough. Suppose an investor commits $10,000 to a project. To consider this a profitable venture, he or she should receive a return *of* capital ($10,000) and a significant return *on* the capital, too. Self-improvement programs should be the same. If you make an investment of time to learn what it has

The point is to get more out of the program than you invest.

to offer, you should expect a future's worth of benefits. That is a favorable cost/benefit analysis.

The Entrepreneur's 12-Step Program won't teach you anything you can't figure out how to do by yourself, but it can accelerate the process so you get there faster. This affects, most of the time favorably, the results you realize from working this program. If given a half-hearted start and retired prematurely to the shelf, the ideas offered will work about as well. But if given your time and thoughtful attention from the beginning, greater possibilities for you can be realized and maintained with ease.

When you start working through the Entrepreneur's 12-Step Program, your entrepreneurial attitude, or small pieces of it, will probably experience some change. As a result, you may see things going on in your business or at the workplace that weren't evident to you—and aren't always positive. Once I commented to friends that my growth was uncomfortable and came with the discovery of "land mines" going off all around. One commented, "That's probably nothing new, but your ability to see them is."

Some realizations about your current circumstances may be appealing and attractive while others seem less so. In either case you can become motivated to turn away from what you don't like to the direction of what you do. Apply something meaningful from one of the 12 steps as a different approach. This is the essence of working through the program. You will likely find yourself contending with results different from anything you've created in the past. That's the point. You learn what the possibilities are so you have more choices. That improves your potential to succeed.

The Entrepreneur's 12-Step Program can alter your attitude so it's more conducive to the successful completion of your entrepreneurial goals. It also complements your existing skills so they can produce more with focused effort. This fine-tuning makes converting a hobby into a business, buying an existing operation, or launching a start-up opportunity much more viable alternatives for you to consider. Whatever you choose, by working these steps you can't help but improve the odds your circumstances will improve. Others have.

Starting is the hardest part of anything.

To make use of the Entrepreneur's 12-Step Program, read through it first at your usual pace, perhaps jotting thoughts and notes in the margins and/or highlight phrases of particular interest or meaning to you.

Next, return to Step 1 and reread it carefully, adding more notes and highlights. The Entrepreneur's 12-Step Program is like a movie you can see five times and each time discover something new. That doesn't happen because the movie has changed; it happens because you have.

As you're rereading, think about how the ideas you encounter can apply to your circumstances. Does the material reveal any truths you like or others you don't? Take all the time you want, too, since this is not a race with anybody. Don't move on to the next step until you can see ways in which the one you've been considering can be applied to your circumstances.

Finding the shadows of your old attitude offers the biggest clues to improvement.

Next, before taking any action, you might solicit input from others about your experiences and the solutions you may be evaluating. This is a good way to broaden your perspective and develop additional options or choices—entrepreneurs always create options. Keep in mind when you ask for an opinion you often get one you may not like. Further, you can't use all that you'll get, either, so be prepared to accept some and rule out others. Then brace yourself for the disappointment of those whose opinions you set aside!

Don't make radical changes when you start to use the program. Don't quit your job, sell your business, or

ERR ON THE SIDE OF CAUTION

borrow a lot of money—yet. Observe first what is going on. Gradually, and gently, then incorporate the wisdom of each step into your endeavors. Work up to the big changes.

Proceed through the various steps as described, developing a good understanding of each as you go along and enough confidence to use them automatically whenever or wherever appropriate. It could take 12 weeks or 12 months. Thereafter you'll perfect your use of the steps to support your efforts daily. Refer to them often for additional guidance. You may come up with a solution or approach that's entirely different from others you tried in the past. Performance—the program is working.

The diagram of The Entrepreneurial Attitude is a visual reminder of the steps in the program. Because it's memorable and memorizable, it becomes a valuable aid in helping you raise your "EQ." By dividing the steps into the categories the diagram depicts, you can emphasize specific parts of your entrepreneurial attitude to work on. For example, when unclear about goals or the future, review Steps 1 through 4. Working with Steps 5 through 7 may ease feelings of complacency. Working with Steps 8 through 12 may deter poor performance and resulting frustration.

Adopting the Entrepreneur's 12-Step Program supports the creation of a new, entrepreneurial lifestyle. Sooner or later successful behaviors evolve. When this happens, you're more likely than ever before to discover success on all the playing fields of life. You will have more freedom to choose which game you want to play. This is the domain of entrepreneurs.

Step 1 follows.

"Vision penetrates the translucence of uncertainty."

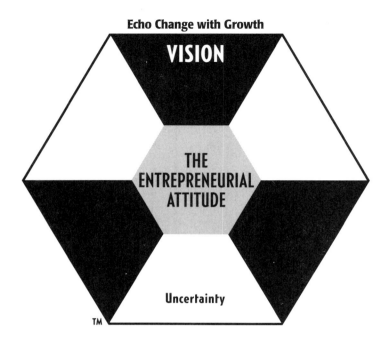

Echo Change with Growth

VISION

THE ENTREPRENEURIAL ATTITUDE

Uncertainty

TM

1. Echo Change with Growth

New results come from new ideas. One of the ways trappers used to capture small monkeys in the jungle takes advantage of a failure to follow this first step. An orange or other similar-sized fruit was placed in a box in the monkeys' territory. Completing the setup, the box had a hole large enough for a monkey's hand to reach through and grasp the fruit. However, the fruit was bigger than the hole, so the small hand clutching it couldn't withdraw. This simple trap worked because the monkeys' desire to hang onto the fruit was so strong they would allow themselves to be captured before letting go.

This story illustrates how tightly (and rashly) we sometimes cling to old attitudes that no longer serve a purpose. The goal of achieving different results could depend on doing different things, but many anonymous entrepreneurs never put this idea into action by letting go of what doesn't work. Yet they are surprised when results do not improve. You can find plenty of examples in the typical workplace where recurring unproductive behaviors remain linked to greater expectations. This happens because most people resist change—it represents the unknown—so they stay with what they know even if it's worse. But how can anything improve if it doesn't change?

To make the transition to entrepreneurship, the first step requires letting go of what no longer serves your purpose. You may find it surprising to discover that we often cling to those things that harm us as tightly as those that help. As a result, developing a sound entrepreneurial attitude can be difficult. Only when you're ready to release aspects of an anonymous entrepreneur's attitude can you begin to change, and growth will be the natural result.

The mechanics of sound offer a good way to describe the action of Step 1. Different types of mammals and reptiles use sound to determine obstacles in the path ahead. To do this they emit a sound that spreads in all directions. The sound travels as waves, and when these hit an object they bounce back to the sender. When decoded, the reflected sound waves paint a picture of what lies ahead. We humans have copied and developed this natural phenomenon into radar and sonar.

Change, for the entrepreneur, can work in a similar wavelike fashion. Cause and effect reveals what happens when you take an action. Waves of energy created by the action expand in the intended direction, affecting whatever is in their path. The entrepreneur observes the effects, interpreting them as good or bad. For example, sales increase because of a new advertising pitch or they don't.

They may respond again with a second overture which, if the same as the original and in the same environment, will likely produce the same result. But if the sender changes to a different strategy, the effect may be different, too. This describes the trial-and-error process, the action of Step 1 as it applies to the successful entrepreneurial attitude.

If actions are consistent with the entrepreneur's vision, then results will be consistent as well. And with foresight and planning they will be favorable. Step 1 of the Entrepreneur's 12-Step Program assumes you want or already have your own business and that you want to improve your financial or business results. This may require adjusting your approach, bringing it in line with a new, entrepreneurial way of thinking. Growth, the echo of change, then will follow.

Despite how desirable, making the transition to entrepreneurship is no cakewalk. I left a successful corporate career to pursue another as an author, publisher, investor, and entrepreneur. My previous employment required me to be assertive, driven, extroverted, and efficient with my time and project management. It was necessary to see the big picture at all times while maintaining a familiarity with the details of many projects and delegating responsibility for them to others. My job was to do one thing: solve problems (usually everyone else's). Thus, I had to maximize time, leverage effort, and move fast.

A new perspective was necessary, though, for my new career choice. Writing is an introspective activity and requires a receptive, patient, balanced state of mind. Keeping thoughts organized as well as creative is important. Word choice and the turn of each phrase affect the meaning (and impact) of the larger message. There is no leverage or delegation, and progress can be frustratingly slow. Periodically shifting pace and perspective is needed to stay fresh. Clearly you can see I had to change my behavior—patience—to produce a change in my results. Imagine my uncertainty about the world of authorship without such adjustments to my attitude. Conversely, imagine the uncertainty of a corporate executive used to the cocktail circuit assuming the attitude and solitary work style of a writer.

Tomorrow's career growth is a reverberation of the changes you make today.

Continue the behaviors of the past and you continue the results. If, however, you generate a different type of wave by emitting actions that support a new vision, the results will be more positive. Following are a few ways you can begin.

MANAGE AND CREATE CHANGE

Change frightens people—it involves risk. Why not remain comfortable then with the status quo? Because business is in constant motion. "Status quo" thus can become a synonym for falling behind, an undesirable course for the person behind that business. We must keep pace with forward-moving competitors and a marketplace that never sleeps. An entrepreneur riding a wave created by the blast of a new idea needs to stay alert to surrounding waves, too. Eventually some will move faster and have more impact. Good ideas soon play out and become obsolete if not improved. That's when the Phase Two Entrepreneurial Growth Wall explained by Dr. Richard Osborne strikes like a tidal wave.

For anonymous entrepreneurs, a growth wall has already sprung up. Uncertainty, complacency, and/or frustration may dominate your attitude. The best way to tear down such growth wall "bricks" is to start altering your behavior. That process begins by overcoming the fear of change, then feelings of uncertainty give way to recognition of what is possible.

When you stop giving attention to thinking that doesn't support successful entrepreneurship, a "behavior vacuum" results. Nature hates a vacuum and will find ways to fill it up. For example, have you ever noticed how you feel drained after an emotional experience? This happens because you've released lots of energy. Here you have an opportunity to fill yourself with something new and positive—in this case, to reinforce your entrepreneurial attitude. Reading one of these steps is a good choice, as would be making a list of the 10 best things about you.

Another benefit of Step 1 is learning to moderate beliefs and behaviors that don't support your emergence as a powerful entrepreneur. Examples include fear of failure, fear of success, procrastination, or paralysis-by-analysis. Strive to put an end to the self-fulfilling prophecies that these become—they keep you anonymous.

Changes beyond our control often result from someone else's creative effort. The owner of your business lays off your department; your banker cancels your credit line; you get sued over a bogus claim; the tax code changes again in your state and for the worse. We have little or no control over such things, so we fear them.

And yet change is the only constant in everyone's life. It makes sense to embrace it.

Changes we can control are often ones we create. For example, you may continue in your present career "as is" or try for another position. Alternatively, you can become a part-time multilevel marketer, start or acquire a small business, or move into another line of work. Many existing opportunities, as well as new ones, can attract entrepreneurs. Some insights will dawn in the middle of the night, so write them down. (Sleep can come later, while good ideas may not.) Ideas create energy and excitement, and help build a positive attitude when they're converted into a doable plan. Entrepreneurs get hooked on that feeling.

START PART-TIME

To know that you can get started as an entrepreneur today without giving up the security of a job relieves much of the fear associated with making the shift.

Part-time involvement offers a practical way to experience entrepreneurship at the entry level with limited risk attached.

Many businesses have their genesis in a hobby or some activity intended for personal enjoyment. Obviously these are performed afterhours, but sometimes recognition of a marketing opportunity allows them to expand. Farming provides one example. *The Wall Street Journal* highlighted this phenomenon in the August 22, 1997, issue stating, "A big reason hobby farms are sprouting in the 1990's is enthusiasts are finding ways to make them pay for themselves, thanks to a growing gourmet demand for fresh, organic foods." Part-time farming can pay for a real estate investment and thus become part-time entrepreneurship.

Alternatively, others start a part-time business with every intention of converting it into a full-time occupation. This is particularly common among professionals who develop a "free-lance" practice on the side until that client base alone can sustain them. Many writers, for example, use this approach. Multilevel marketers do the same. So do real estate investors.

My best client ever was a professional wallpaper hanger from southern California. He was so good he worked in the homes of all the Hollywood movie stars—a market that he cultivated. Over the course of several years this man started buying investment real estate through me in southern Missouri and also in Texas. He made his inspection trips on weekends and worked on his properties, by long distance, during the evenings. Eventually, through several acquisitions, he was able to count on a substantial monthly income and retire. He did very well as a part-time entrepreneur.

Industries where part-time entrepreneurship presents a viable alternative are simply too numerous to mention. In fact, part-time entrepreneurship may be today's incubator and testing ground for tomorrow's success stories.

LEARN BY OBSERVING Often you can learn to manage this process of change more easily if you follow an example set by other successful entrepreneurs. That is, you can identify things they do that seem to contribute favorably to their success. Pick out successful entrepreneurs in your area and notice how they operate—at least one exists behind every thriving business. Talk to several if possible. Not only can you learn a great deal in this way, but when confronted with difficult situations you can simply ask yourself what you believe these models would do. Then do that.

My parents were entrepreneurs who started an engineering company from scratch. Their office was in our dining room and their production area fit in the basement. They also raised me, three brothers, and one sister—five kids; maintained a good home plus a place at the lake; took plenty of trips; and lived very well. Eventually they put an office building behind our house, and through its windows they got to watch their business, family, and garden grow. Mom and Dad were a success on their terms and pretty good fishermen, too. That's true entrepreneurship. Perhaps it's no surprise that all five of their kids became entrepreneurs as well.

Today I think of my parents when confronted with a tough challenge. I imagine what they would do in my circumstances and then I do that. Even if they aren't present with me, their wisdom is.

Learning by observation also provides a practical solution to management problems. I was once the equivalent of a franchisee for a national company. We had regional vice presidents and district sales managers to help us maintain our relationship with the franchiser and improve our business performance. They were sort of like a boss.

Eventually I was offered the job of national sales manager, the one who supervises and is responsible for all the regional vice presidents and the district sales managers. By taking this position I would become my boss's boss—a difficult transition. I was 32 with seven years' experience in real estate. My new subordinates ranged from 36 to 62, and none had less than 10 years' experience. This was a challenge.

Words of encouragement came from the California regional vice president, who has since become a very close friend. On my first field trip with him, he said, "Okay, you have been selected to be the boss and I don't know why, because so many have more experience than you. But there must be something about you that qualifies you for your position. Let me help you find out what it is." He did.

I was able to observe this man in action and see all the other regional vice presidents up close and personal, too. I learned what they did that worked and communicated those solutions to all other members of field management. We leveraged our answers. Gradually improvements came, and with them some respect for this young upstart from southern Missouri.

IMITATE AND INVENT

There are two types of creativity that can strengthen the architecture of your entrepreneurial attitude. The first involves imitation and is called *imitative entrepreneurship,* simply the act of mimicking what someone else has done successfully elsewhere. Read history—it's full of solutions others have used for the problems of an earlier day. Since history repeats itself, you may discover existing applications for new challenges as well. Travel, surf the Net, and expose yourself to a variety of information about things and happenings in other areas.

Today, franchising is probably the most common form of imitative entrepreneurship. This huge industry derives entirely from the concept of imitation; that is, selling a proven concept to others who in turn can succeed by imitating it in their chosen locale. If this sounds like your niche, consider your options within the over 2,000 different franchises you can choose from. Pick one out, buy it, and go to work. Instant imitative entrepreneurship.

Inventive entrepreneurship, the second form of creativity, is more special and often rare. This type of entrepreneurship occurs when instinct, intellect, and experience collide and a totally new idea emerges. It's powerful stuff, perhaps more often recognizable in the work of artists we admire. For example, Picasso attached a bicycle handle to a bicycle seat and called the result "Toro." Shifting into entrepreneurial mode, once upon a time two businesspersons were brainstorming for a new product. One was thinking of time and the other of music. A clock radio became the offspring of their creativity and millions were sold, a prime example of inventive entrepreneurship.

I attempted to develop imitative and inventive entrepreneurship as a resource in my franchise company. We formed a small brainstorming group—dubbed "Genesis"—to meet weekly and search for new ideas to improve business results. All discussions were confidential, and there was no rank in the room except for the smell of an occasional bad idea. We did not soothe each other's egos, either, when a really bad idea belly-flopped into conversation. Instead, we made good-natured fun of the idea and each other, eliminating any sense of pressure to produce only brilliant points when we spoke. We found that the weak ideas frequently led us to the powerful ones. This open atmosphere encouraged complete participation.

To further release our creative juices in Genesis we emphasized laughter, a very healthy stimulant. People work better when they're having a good time. We kicked off our shoes during those meetings and never discussed new ideas until each of us blew off steam about the aggravation of the day. Sometimes we would go on this way for 90 percent of the allotted meeting time and then discover remarkable results surfacing in the last 10 percent of the get-together. On more than one occasion we each stood alone on the conference room table, raising our arms overhead and shouting "I'm depressed!" three times. You cannot do this in front of anyone else, no matter how down you are, and not laugh.

As a result of all these antics, Genesis evolved as an intensely powerful entrepreneurial influence. Many concepts we developed there produced favorable business results and are still in use years later. A nationally recognized "Genesis" award was created and presented annually to reward the most proficient use of creativity or marketing in business by any person affiliated with the company. It is coveted. Genesis became the seed for imitative and inventive entrepreneurship in my company.

As an entrepreneur you should recognize that imitative and inventive entrepreneurship are valuable assets. They contribute to your business's base of intellectual capital—the power within a business to correctly identify opportunities and create solutions to take advantage of them. Intellectual capital also refers to the health and moral fiber of the corporate culture an entrepreneur creates. It is a reflection of the entrepreneur's entrepreneurial attitude. When a business is sold, intellectual capital is converted to tangible wealth—money—in the form of a sales price. All this comes from creativity, the source.

The first step does not tell you or anyone else how to change. That's left for you and them to decide. This step suggests that if you want something different from your current career choice, the changes you need to make begin with your attitude. Adjustments here have the potential to echo far into your future as growth.

Overcome fear of change by managing it. To be more powerful, create it.

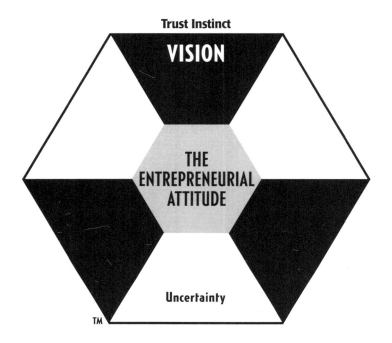

Trust Instinct

VISION

THE ENTREPRENEURIAL ATTITUDE

Uncertainty

TM

2. TRUST INSTINCT

Fake it till you make it. Many people think first impressions form 90 percent of our opinions. Everything we learn after receiving a first impression thus may be an effort to confirm what we think we already know. If so this brings new relevance to the power of first impressions, or *instinct,* as a guiding force in our lives. Indeed, this source of information is seldom wrong.

When an opportunity presents itself, instinct helps us quickly recognize it and evaluate how we feel about it. This is a useful tool for entrepreneurs, who look at lots of opportunities, and thus why it's the second step on the road to developing a strong entrepreneurial attitude.

Instinct is undeniably a powerful force. Animals large and small have thrived for millions of years by relying on instinct to manage their lives. Before evolving the capacity for complex rational thought, our ancestors weren't much different. We've all survived by tapping into this valuable resource.

BEFRIEND AN OLD COMPANION

In his book *Dragons of Eden,* Dr. Carl Sagan suggested instinct might spring from a genetic memory imprinted in our minds through eons of experience. This collection of ancient information still actively influences our behaviors, strengths, and fears. This may explain why so many people share an instinctive fear of reptiles—an old reminder that they once had us for dinner.

Carl Jung, the famous Swiss psychologist, proposed that instinctive thoughts might be messages from our unconscious. These messages come in the form of myths and dreams. So, by Dr. Jung's way of thinking, to hear and understand instinct we learn to interpret the language of myth and dreams. We might also regard instinct such as this the "collective unconscious" or the subconscious mind in action. It is constantly combining information to form conclusions that we recognize as a new awareness or flash of insight.

Many benefits arise from of trusting your instinct. One is the sense that your entrepreneurial vision is correct, which instills confidence, when obstacles appear. Instinct helps entrepreneurs stay focused and on track, too, when others may stray.

Confidence and focus strengthen your entrepreneurial attitude; instinct helps it grow.

It's possible to put instinct to work as a part of your entrepreneurial attitude. First learn to hear it better. Then become more familiar with and confident in what it nudges you to do. Eventually when you hear that inner voice you will take notice, then action. That can improve your attitude as well as your business performance.

After working at the headquarters of my company

for two years, I wanted and requested a raise. I was offered a choice between a fixed increase in salary or a percentage of the improvement in business results that might occur. My boss told me to take my time and think about it for a few days. I sat quietly for about 10 seconds and then made my choice entirely by instinct. He was surprised I acted so quickly. He was also surprised when my choice earned me $10,000 more than the alternative.

Instinctive messages like this one come fast and with clarity. They may be stimulated by almost anything at any time. When you receive one of these personal telegrams it has an unmistakable quality of truth, leaving nothing to question. When you know, you know. Write your instinctive thoughts down to preserve them in their purest form. These may represent seeds of opportunity for your transition to entrepreneurship today or in the future.

Instinct can also help reduce uncertainty, which is especially powerful when linked to compatible skills. A Bedouin living in the desert stopped at an oasis for the night. He was going to leave his camel while he went in for refreshment but was afraid it would run away. On the other hand, he was concerned that in tying the camel up, Allah might be offended by his lack of faith that the animal would remain. Concerned, the traveler sought the advice of a local wise man, who said, "Trust in Allah and tie up your camel."

DO MORE RESEARCH The point of the preceding story is that even though instinct is strong, you can complement it and make it work even better. Just because instinct has indicated your projects would come to fruition doesn't mean you stop working—the feeling is based on continued effort.

You might plan projects in which the right instinct does not come. This doesn't signal a dead-end; it means your subconscious mind, or instinct, doesn't have enough information to form a definitive opinion. Conduct more research by questioning your objectives, reevaluating the way you plan to achieve them. Search for errors of commission (those things you do that are wrong) and errors of omission (those things you should have done but left out of the process). Most of all, solicit objective opinions to ensure your plans are realistic.

When I wrote my first book about business valuation, I did so against my "rational" judgment. Some people thought it was unrealistic and a waste of time. My confidence and focus prevailed, though, because I trusted my instinct and was familiar with my market.

When I finished the book, I sent it to all the national franchise company training directors and offered to do one-day seminars for their affiliates. Century 21, largest of all, inquired for more information. Imagine my excitement! When asked about the cost, I said my seminar was so good that if they would pay my expenses, I would waive my normal fee and do one free to demonstrate the quality of my product. I had never been paid as much as $10 to talk to anybody about anything. Imagine my fear! After the first seminar, they promptly started booking more . . . and paid my normal fee, too.

Afterward, while in Los Angeles conducting a seminar, I was contacted by the new president of United Farm Agency, the company with which I had been affiliated previously. He offered me a position as the national vice president of sales, which I later accepted.

The Anonymous Entrepreneur was born out of instinct, too. Originally it was a chapter in a major revision of my earlier book on business valuations. The concept represented an idea I felt was important but deserved greater attention. And I just could not let it go because of its deep ring of truth with so many others and me. Now it's a book.

I researched my new topic by reviewing my expe-

Research developed my instinct. Instinct developed my confidence. Confidence brought me opportunity.

rience with the many real estate entrepreneurs I had trained and supported during the previous decade. I talked to entrepreneurs about their experiences and found the topic of the entrepreneurial attitude was a common denominator to all their experiences. I explored the Internet looking for information about the entrepreneurial attitude and searched in bookstores for material describing the importance of and how to build the entrepreneurial attitude. I found little to nothing. My instincts had led me to an opportunity. Afterward, I prepared spreadsheets to inform myself of the risks, costs, and rewards of book publishing. I even sent rough manuscripts to a score of entrepreneurs and professionals all over the country to read and help me define the target markets. All this was done before spending any money. Research confirmed the direction of my instinct, which in turn pressed me forward during the year it took to build *The Anonymous Entrepreneur.*

GET READY FOR A RIDE When you allow an entrepreneurial attitude to emerge, it can create chaos in your career. People you work with may expect you to behave a certain way, but then you change because instinct leads you to try new approaches to old problems. Often this shift is interpreted as changing the rules of your relationships and may be met with resistance, isolation, and even termination of your employment or your career. You may have to leave associates, too. These things happen because you want something different. Instinct helps you discover what to do and when to take action, but it's also the power that will see you through the transition from where you're leaving to where you want to go.

When attempting to heed the advice of your instinct, try to avoid drastic action. Change occurs by degrees. Time is yours to take. Following one's instinct can become a difficult and challenging proposition, not so much because of what it tells you to do, but because of what it doesn't. Many times you'll want—or need—an answer to a question and want it now. In these instances, until the answer comes—clearly—don't move. Research and wait for the wisdom of instinct's voice. If it stays silent, that's a sign the timing or some other element is not right. When the gong sounds, you will know.

CULTIVATE YOUR CONFIDENCE

You can learn cues to stimulate your instinct. Eastern philosophies promote meditation as a device to hear the words of an inner voice. Author and Jungian analyst Robert Johnson has suggested a similar approach in his book *She.* He proposed that the feminine psyche has the ability to find healing and answers by remaining very still for as long as is necessary.

My instinct often reveals itself at times when the static of external interference is low. I get my best ideas driving home from work, in the shower, while practicing yoga, or when working in my yard or wood shop. At these times my mind is free to make new thought connections, turning apparently absurd possibilities into plausible realities.

Another way you can prime your instinct pump is with questions. Write down a question about a certain issue and then forget it. Our brains have the power to monitor and maintain our bodies, the most complex machines we know. Our minds can create powerful, intricate dreams when we aren't even awake. Turn over your questions to these amazing resources and as they simmer unconsciously, your answers will float to the top. Take a few minutes from your reading now and think about where your instinct speaks most frequently. Write out a question or two if you wish.

It's also possible to refine your instinct by drawing a picture of a concept or idea you want to try. List associated ideas that make it clearer. Next, take at look at all the associated words and start to prioritize them. Some will "feel" better than others will, so move them to the top of the list. Do this entirely on the basis of what you *feel,* not what you think. Try it when planning your next round of advertising, building a case for a raise, modifying how you do your work, or acting on anything else that's important to your career. In the end instinct will have helped flesh out a concept to expand your business opportunities.

Some consider instinct a form of divine guidance. I once shared with a friend my experience that the only thing wrong with my instinct was my failure to listen and act accordingly, because it was always right. My friend suggested I consider calling it by another name—higher power—and I've had greater confidence in it ever since.

Sometimes instinct's advice makes no sense. That's when you have the greatest opportunity to learn to trust it, a valuable asset when managing a career as an entrepreneur. When I'm involved in a business deal with a pending conclusion, I question myself about whether things will turn out as I have planned. Even though I frequently get a fast answer, I never expect it. If the reply doesn't appear right away, it may come later. I don't move until it does, though, because these answers are always right for me.

When I get a confirmation from my instinct it feels like the slightest sense of relief in my stomach. Maybe you experience this sort of "gut feeling," too. Don't question it. Based on that tiniest of feelings I've stretched my resources past the red line and have known others who've done the same. I have borrowed well over a million dollars when it made no business sense because my instinct told me to take the plunge. It was the right move, too. Instinct is my—and your— best guide.

Instinct can illuminate the differences between one entrepreneur versus another. This is a valuable asset to establish and maintain. The more skillfully you extrapolate these differences in entrepreneurial atti-tude into business strategies, the greater your poten-tial to profit with something others don't have. Business results can and will improve. Drawing out what is unique about your entrepreneurial attitude and imprinting it upon a business can make you more successful than operating according to other stan-dards of lesser importance, too. Entrepreneurs' one-of-a-kind belief systems determine what they can and will do best, and instinct helps you confidently recog-nize what these are.

Instinct maneuvers you into position to become a magnet for entrepreneurship and success. With Step 2 you can develop and use instinct as a tool to improve your entrepreneurial attitude. Then imagine what you envision is already true and act accordingly. Fake it till you make it. Your job is to create a vision of you—entrepreneur. How does it feel? Good? It's working.

Entrepreneurs don't want to be a carbon copy of anyone else— they are origi-nals.

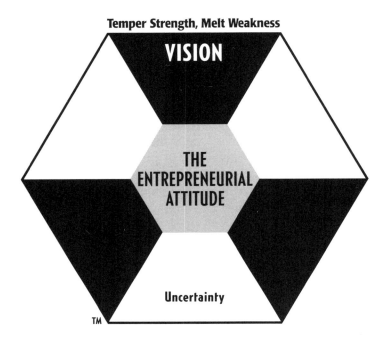

Temper Strength, Melt Weakness

VISION

THE ENTREPRENEURIAL ATTITUDE

Uncertainty

TM

3. TEMPER STRENGTH, MELT WEAKNES

What makes you good makes you bad. Milton Erickson was a well-known psychologist wh illustrates the power of paradox with a childhoo story. As a young boy he lived on a farm with his fam ily. One day he was observing his father trying to lea a young bull out of the barn. The father was pulling o a rope around the neck of the bull, who was resistin as bulls are prone to do. Young Milton, watching thi suggested his father try another approach. Taking th rope, Milton gently turned the bull 180 degrees so was facing into the barn. Then he started pulling th rope once more. Naturally, the bull resisted again an backed out of the barn.

You have as much potential to become a successf entrepreneur as anyone else—and it's up to you to di cover and release that potential. Many times, though, you discover your best resources may be working to your disadvantage. The greatest benefit of tackling Step 3 is learning to diminish the influence of an attitude that short-circuits your transition to entrepreneurship.

Step 1 taught finding the opportunity in business by looking for problems that create a need. Step 2 encouraged trusting your instinct. The next step involves learning to navigate successfully through a career in entrepreneurship successfully when unfavorable influences are removed. Because at some point strengths can actually become weaknesses, developing a reliable awareness of this phenomenon helps you look at yourself more objectively. When you notice how your strengths and weaknesses work for or against you, you can apply moderation to your responses and transform a problem into a useful solution.

Practice moderation by doing half as much as you want. If necessary you can do more later.

WHEN MY BEST BECOMES MY WORST

Many weaknesses derive from an overextension of a strength, often the point of origin for trouble. Results get short-circuited by an excessive dependency on certain perceived strengths and that creates a problem. To locate weaknesses you first must come to know your strengths and when you lean on them most. The more dominant a strength, the more suspicious you can be of it as a trouble source. The process begins by examining the only thing you can really change—yourself.

In the history of the United States lies an obvious example of how a strength can turn into a problem. Taxation was originally intended as a means to finance the infrastructure needed to build a country. Little by little, however, the American tax code has shifted from these constructive beginnings to a more destructive process. For example, according to the

National Commission on Economic Growth and Tax Reform:

- The current tax code is 7,000,000+ words long; Lincoln's Gettysburg address has 269 words, and the Declaration of Independence 1,337 words.
- The IRS's "simplest" return, the EZForm 1040, has 33 pages of instructions. American business will spend 3.4 billion hours, and individuals 1.7 billion hours, simply trying to comply with the tax code. That's equivalent to a "staff" of 3 million people working full time, year-round, just on taxes.
- All of this costs our economy $200 billion each year. It's like taking every new car, van, and truck General Motors builds in a year and dumping them into the ocean.
- The IRS is twice as big as the CIA and five times the size of the FBI, plus it controls more information about individual Americans than any other agency.

This is the government's solution to help us determine how much in taxes we owe annually. It is also a prime example of a strength transformed into a weakness—government behavior that needs to be modified with a return to the simple intentions of the original tax system.

Another example of a strength becoming a weakness in business is the common practice of comparing the business and its employees to a "family." Beware when forming a relationship with companies that aggressively promote this theme.

Clearly, developing a strong sense of team spirit and commitment to a common goal is important and a valuable business asset. And when business results are favorable, the feeling of togetherness or unity feels kind of like being part of a family. Overuse of the "family theme," however, may signal weak leadership that won't address the issues of poor business results or inefficiency created by problem employees—it's easier to say being part of the family means accepting these things. In such instances employees may respond less favorably to family references and harbor increased, albeit silent, resentment. They come to work for the challenge, the creative opportunities, and the money, not the family feeling that once may have been a strength but now has soured with poor business results and become a weakness.

Without vigilance, it's easy to fall into reacting without thinking about the appropriateness of the response. For example, during a behavioral science experiment, a German shepherd was placed in a wire cage and then a painful electrical shock was delivered. The dog yelped and became submissive. This same sequence played out a few more times and each produced the same reaction. Next, the dog was moved to a different cage and setting. This time a small, almost imperceptible, electrical shock was delivered. The dog, however, reacted as if the charge was as powerful as those given earlier. Minimum stimulus—maximum response.

Excessive dependencies on strengths often occur in response to small stimuli.

We sometimes overreact to the challenges of a transition to entrepreneurship. It can create lots of stress and feel like the most difficult part of becoming an entrepreneur. We need to govern ourselves better. For example, don't spend too much time and money attempting to launch an idea. Unrealistic expectations born of excessive excitement have created many failures. People with too much money and not enough commitment often make this mistake: they spend their money before figuring out if the investment is worthwhile.

Be realistic about the excitement of entrepreneurship.

The idea that a weakness may actually be an overextension of a strength is not new. Carl Jung suggested people have personality types so distinct they may be present at birth. Building on this theory, Dr. Paul Mok has advanced into the workplace with a more practical description of such types and a test to determine

TYPES OF STRENGTH AND WEAKNESS

them under normal conditions versus stress. The four personality types Mok described are the Thinker, Intuitor, Feeler, and Sensor.

When discussing personality types, no judgment should be made about the value of any of them. They all have their place in the world, and none is any better or more effective than any other. The best one for us is the one that enables us to get the best results from what we have to offer. Nor are we all one type or another. Typically we're mixtures, with one personality type more dominant than others.

An individual can assess his or her mix of communicating styles by taking a self-administered survey developed and copyrighted by Dr. Mok. It is called the "Survey of Communicating Styles" and provides data on your primary style of relating under favorable conditions as well as how you may shift loads under stress conditions (see Bibliography).

Thinkers have a plod-horse mentality that pushes them to move ahead at a slow, step-by-step pace. They respond favorably to analytical information and arguments. They are the bureaucratic influence that is needed in every company to keep it moving on an even keel.

Intuitors deal in the currency of intellectual capital. They are good at brainstorming for new solutions to old problems as well as charismatic and receptive to the world of possibilities. They also respond favorably to creative challenges, which makes them very valuable when positioned as entrepreneurs.

Feelers respond to life in terms of their emotions. Their modus operandi includes showering their emotions wherever they go, which can make them an inspiring influence in business. You will usually like a Feeler, since it's frequently his or her mission to make sure you do.

Sensors do not know a thing until it makes direct contact through their senses. As children they must touch everything. This dynamic aspect of their personality drives Sensors to become the movers and shakers of the world. They can grow up to be leaders in business and politics—or convicts. They take action, fast, and can be terrific entrepreneurs.

Each of these four personality types has distinctive strengths. Stress may trigger them to short-circuit as they look for ways to compensate. During difficult times it is natural to do what you know and depend on a strength to get you through. When taken to extremes by overreacting, through, the result can be a poison pill instead of a solution.

When a Thinker's attitude short-circuits, for example, she or he starts thinking too much and gets paralysis-by-analysis. These people get into arguments with themselves, which neutralizes their decision-making capability. No action will occur. An excessive dependency on a strength thus becomes a weakness.

The Intuitor's greatest strength is his or her vision. This attribute becomes a weakness when it's not balanced by actions, analysis of the impact of actions, and revised actions. In a word, accountability. Intuitors left unaccountable can detach themselves from a performance orientation and exist in a daydream world filled with wonderful visions that never become reality. A strength thereby becomes a weakness.

Feelers turn up the volume of their emotions when attempting to make a point that isn't getting across. They display emotional reactions to provoke a response. This strength, when used to excess, might cause a person to appear insincere. People become suspicious of the Feeler's motives. As a result, they have a more difficult time building consensus or team spirit—their strength becomes a weakness.

When Sensors depend excessively on their strength, they will appear to have gone wild. They already move faster and farther in a day than most people do in a week. Accelerate that pace and intended objectives don't have a chance to occur before the Sensor has headed off in a new direction. Failing to stay connected to the army often leaves them alone in the middle of the battlefield. They can't win without teamwork, which is crippled when their strength becomes a weakness.

I am an Intuitor/Sensor, able to develop new ideas and make them happen. But these strengths cause me a problem when I take on too many projects at once. As a result, I get less than the best results with each and am often overworked. Moderation for me is patience. This helps me pace myself, prioritize, and improve my entrepreneurship as an author, investor, and consultant.

IDEA PUT TO USE Now let's be practical. You can make Step 3 work for you by doing three things.

First, take responsibility for your attitude. Nobody can make you act the way you do but you. Observe other people's patterns of behavior and you start to see your own more clearly. How do they react to certain situations? How do you? How do they react to you? How do you react to them? Observing the things other people do also provides a great way to learn what is consistent with your beliefs and what is not. This tactic can help you get to know your entrepreneurial self quite well. Step out and go beyond who or what is causing a problem and look at your own role first. Until you do and stop reacting, it's possible someone else is controlling you.

Second, identify your greatest strength—the one right under your nose that's a source of hidden pride. Realize this might be your greatest weakness, too. In the examples of personality types presented earlier, the excessive dependency on a strength made the anonymous entrepreneur weak and out of control.

Often we miss what's wrong because we're looking for a weakness rather than a strength.

Finally, maintain an awareness of how your strength can short-circuit your entrepreneurial attitude and transition to entrepreneurship. Awareness is 90 percent of solving any problem. Open your eyes to honestly recognize weaknesses and they can start to disappear. With a more moderate style, previously maintained results are free to improve.

Take control of your behaviors and attitude. View your strengths as potential weaknesses, and accept they could be creating a problem for you. Step 3 offers a productive new reality. You can now see what is needed to improve yourself and your circumstances. Uncertainty will fade as self-perceptions improve. Entrepreneurs using Step 3 know what they want and what they have to do to get it. You can return to the wisdom and power of this step anytime to work your way through a problem. It's part of your life and your transition to entrepreneurship.

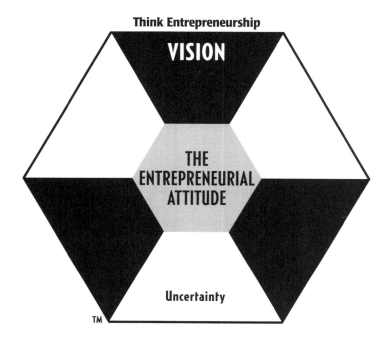

Think Entrepreneurship

VISION

THE
ENTREPRENEURIAL
ATTITUDE

Uncertainty

TM

4. THINK ENTREPRENEURSHIP

The opportunity of a lifetime comes along every 45 days.

Entrepreneurs use opportunity to become successful, and to them, there's never a shortage of opportunity. Failing to recognize stepping-stones is one reason more people don't become entrepreneurs. Developing this ability raises your EQ and can make a significant contribution to your entrepreneurial transition. Entrepreneurs keep their eyes—and minds—open to all possibilities, thus improving their chances of finding one to take advantage of. This is called "thinking entrepreneurship."

As a beginning real estate agent I was advised to "think real estate." It wasn't until reading Marshall Field's famous quote, "Under all is the land," though, that I did. Thereafter I was alert to opportunity everywhere, with the only variables being time, price, and terms. The real estate brokerage experience became one of looking for a better investment opportunity among an unlimited supply.

This lesson was reinforced in me years later by a true American legend. I was a business broker attempting to sell a fiberglass manufacturing plant that built a product, it seemed to me, that would be a perfect acquisition candidate for Wal-Mart. Knowing the quickest way to the CEO is through the executive secretary, I called Sam Walton's office and asked to speak with that person. Then I asked if she could get a description of my offering to Mr. Walton if I sent it to her by overnight mail. She agreed.

The next day I called back and was immediately connected to Sam Walton. He couldn't have been nicer, listening to my brief pitch and then saying, "Chad, I appreciate the call, but I've got all the opportunity I can handle just building new stores." Clearly, his opportunities were better than what I had to show him but on the chance I might have had something good, too, he listened. Entrepreneurs are like this. They want to know about all the deals available and have as many options as possible.

Tune In the Opportunity Channel

Imagine the results you could produce by working twice as efficiently as you already do. Thinking entrepreneurship makes this possible. Tuning your attention to the opportunity channel becomes effortless and highly productive. As a result of this subtle adjustment, incoming information filters through an entrepreneurial lens. You find yourself asking if everything could be an opportunity. And if so, how good an opportunity might each be. Instead of normal working hours, you start leveraging downtime to improve your recognition.

Here's an example of how others have used this concept to their advantage. In real estate franchising, I observed that new agents needed help with their listing skills. They were missing opportunities to list property because they were not cognizant of them and didn't know how to capitalize on them when they were.

A failure to "think listing" means opportunities to capture a property during off-hours can be missed. Naturally, if agents don't see these opportunities, they can't take advantage of them; further, if they do happen to see one but don't know how to develop it, they lose out as well. This limits access to listings that are easy to get. Anyone can do easy work and very often does, which is why competition for these properties is fierce. And why success cut short by what agents simply don't see or can't do anything about is frustrating. As explained in The Entrepreneurial Attitude model, here uncertainty prevails.

Normally real estate agents have little time to develop the first lead because it's often unexpected and occurs at the car wash, in the grocery store, or after church. First the agent must get the prospect's attention and then secure an appointment to develop it into a business opportunity—a listing. Our new agents didn't "think listing" or view their entire world as an opportunity. They also needed better preparation to respond quickly to any inquiry, regardless of where or when it occurred. To help them do this, we created and taught a three-minute listing presentation.

Our approach involved intense training. Sellers all want to sell for the highest price in the shortest time for the least effort. We built an emphasis on our ability to meet these three priorities and summarized information to convey that ability into a three-minute listing drill. Agents practiced delivering this message in front of their mirrors, in role plays, in front of groups, and on videotape. We even had a national competition to determine who could deliver the best three-minute pitch.

By making it easy to respond to a seller's interest,

agents were confidently prepared. They could field an inquiry 24 hours a day. As a result they became listing tigers and doubled their performance compared to others who did not attend the training. By learning to "think listing," their marketplace became a giant opportunity. Thinking entrepreneurship is no different.

Cultivating a constant awareness that searches for needs and then supplying realistic solutions is much of what it takes to be a success. You live and practice Step 4 by constantly asking yourself three simple questions: Where is there a need? What will it take to fill it? Is the solution realistic? Answering these is the key to locating, evaluating, and developing business opportunities, the vehicle to move from anonymity to notoriety.

WHERE IS THERE A NEED?

Recalling my effort to help real estate agents "think listing" reminds me of one who illustrated the point particularly well. She was new and taking over an existing office that had not listed many properties. She did not believe it was possible to build the type and size of listing inventory we suggested she could. Not surprisingly, neither did her predecessor or competitors. Still, many property owners in the area had a need to sell. This agent was unsure of her ability to interest them until she came to work with my company.

I taught her our three-minute listing drill. When practicing she could hardly do the role plays. She was too afraid to go before a video camera with an audience, so we asked everyone else to leave the classroom. Later her confidence grew when the class gave her a standing ovation after viewing her tape. Then she set a realistic listing goal, no longer thinking about what couldn't be done, and went to work.

In four months our new agent secured over 90 listings. All but one was an exclusive, which, for those unfamiliar with the real estate business, is the best kind. She even placed in the finals of a national listing contest. This entrepreneur found a need, decided to try and fill it . . . and did.

Any approach to entrepreneurship involves searching for a gap to parlay it into an opportunity.

Do what everyone else does and do it better, or do something others don't do at all.

For example, how many times have you been disgusted with poor service from a business? You cannot be displeased if you don't have a vision of something better and more satisfying. When this happens you have discovered, at an unexpected time and place, a business opportunity. You can offer the same or similar service of better quality as the basis for creating income.

Opportunities don't approach with flags waving to announce their arrival. Typically they look like problems—a price is too high; the merchandise takes too long to arrive; the service doesn't satisfy. Here is a chance to lower the price and emphasize volume (Wal-Mart), reduce delivery time (Federal Express), or improve service and up the ante to the competition (Land's End). More often than not the genesis of a successful business lies in a glitch that can be fixed. Find yourself a problem. It's based on a need. That's an opportunity.

What Will It Take to Fill a Need?

To consider filling a need, confine your thoughts to how it might be done (or done better). Don't be too concerned yet with the specifics of developing a new product/service or improving something that already exists; the objective is to bring definition to what *might* be done—to clarify a vision.

Returning to the previous example of the new real estate agent, the source of her vision lay outside of herself. She could not fill the need of many existing sellers and expect to fare any better than her competitors by doing only what they also did. She elected to do something different, which was why she joined our franchise program. Thus, her success was inspired by an outside influence or point of view—an important chess piece to control.

Objectivity is an important tool for entrepreneurs, so they collect information from many places. They read, allow their curiosity to roam, travel, and always look for things done elsewhere that could be transported back home. Haven't you ever gone to a unique store or eaten at a special restaurant that has no equal back where you live? These could be opportunities for you to consider. The franchise industry is built on this premise.

One of the most successful entrepreneurs I know turns to cab drivers as primary information sources when he visits a new city. They know what's in the news and often can relay quick updates on the local business climate. This omnivorous appetite for "what's going on" causes most entrepreneurs to have more trouble taking advantage of the many opportunities they find than finding an opportunity to take.

Once a need has crystallized into a vision, the challenge of developing it into a business opportunity takes a new direction. Your proposed solution has to be measured and evaluated. Be realistic.

Is the Solution Realistic?

There's always a chance an opportunity will not produce. If this happens, you can lose precious time and resources that might have been more fruitful applied elsewhere instead. That can be costly when attempting to make the transition from a job to a business.

When you're just starting out, there's little margin for error. It may be wiser to turn down an exciting but uncertain idea in favor of the smaller sure thing. (The time for greater risk will come.) Determining the resources needed to support your vision is worth taking the time to be accurate. Identifying why a product isn't offered or a service isn't better often reveals many things. For example, though it may be possible

Small mistakes in the transition to entrepreneurship can be deadly.

to build the product, will it be affordable? And if it is affordable, will customers pay the cost? Or what if people don't know they have a need for your product? Can you spend enough to change the impressions of an entire market?

Besides money and resources, consider whether you'll find filling a certain need enjoyable. Humans never do anything better than what we enjoy doing the most, so it's likely that what you enjoy is the area where you can succeed most. If creating and maintaining a certain vision does not sound pleasurable for you, don't do it.

A friend of mine is a natural entrepreneur—he likes to start new things. He started his own business providing a service for homes and loved the work. Now, three years later, he's very successful and the business has grown substantially. But his job has changed. Currently he spends most of his time training new employees, but training others to do things he's already done is not his first choice.

As my friend considers expansion plans, he wisely recognizes the need to think about what an aggressive growth strategy will require from him: specifically, more training of people who will train others. This isn't where he wants to go. He has decided to find someone to replace him in this capacity and stick to the innovative aspects of business that he loves most. This is a very significant move because it means he is letting go of what he has been doing. Many entrepreneurs cannot do this, and it becomes a limitation. This man can, and thus he has no limitations.

Once you take on the mind-set offered in Step 4, you'll become open 24 hours a day to the possibility of an unfulfilled need. In fact, once you leave work, the opportunities really surface. Review the day's events on the drive home—which is a good time and place for ideas to surface while still fresh in your mind. Think about opportunity when you're in a different setting, such as your garden, or when you're doing something else that is relaxing. See what happens. And remember, the smallest, simplest ideas are often the very best. Everybody owns a paper clip. Go figure.

"Excitement dissolves complacency."

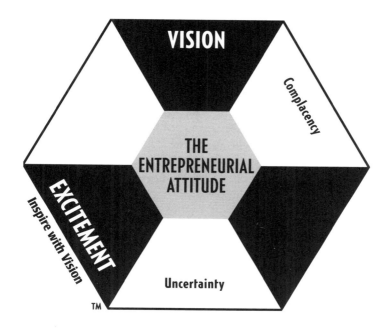

The diagram shows a hexagon with labels: VISION, Complacency, THE ENTREPRENEURIAL ATTITUDE, EXCITEMENT, Inspire with Vision, Uncertainty, TM

5. INSPIRE WITH VISION

In a poem by Samuel Taylor Coleridge, a man falls asleep to dream that he has a conversation with God. After asking the man what he's made of his life, God invites him to share his dreams. When he finishes, the man is then told to imagine his dreams have taken the form of a rose that God gives him. Upon awakening, the man discovers the rose is still in his hand. "Ah, what then?" muses the poet, "What then?"

Entrepreneurs depend on dreams.

Entrepreneurs depend on dreams that are the point of origin for ideas they convert into opportunity. Your dreams are no different. Imagine what it will be like when you have made a successful transition to entrepreneurship. Once you have a vision, you know to apply your knowledge of the marketplace and determine whether the idea is financially feasible. In other words, "Will anybody want this idea, and can it be delivered for a profit?" If all systems are "go," you have a concept that can create excitement. It will inspire you and any others that may get involved, helping your idea take flight. Your vision will illuminate the pathways you've chosen to follow.

Steps 1 through 4 of the Entrepreneur's 12-Step Program help determine the correct path to a goal. Steps 8 to 12 eliminate operational obstacles, decrease resistance, and improve an entrepreneur's ability to perform.

Steps 5, 6, and 7—the center of the program— focus attention on releasing your passion for freedom through the vehicle of entrepreneurship. This internal drive makes entrepreneurs care about their work enough to do whatever it takes to succeed. Excitement and inspiration born of good vision establish the emotional link between recognition and performance that will help beat the odds against you.

THE POWER OF VISION

Vision is a power tool in your transition to entrepreneurship. Without the impetus of a vision, complacency can gradually undermine an entrepreneurial attitude. Have you ever seen a business succeed long term with employees or an owner who didn't care? It's the responsibility of the lead entrepreneur to define, establish, and share the vision. This step takes courage, because it's a commitment to a goal—but that's why it's so inspiring.

In my real estate franchise company, I established a new vision for our company, employees, and franchisees. I literally drew them a picture in words by dating a "vision memo" several years in the future. This communiqué proceeded to explain what had changed in the company in the past several years—before it actually happened. It was an interesting approach.

My vision was very aggressive and some thought not possible. To be honest, it was, but it needed to be.

I found over the months that followed, though, that more people liked having a vision to work toward. The content was actually less important than having a picture of something they wanted to become a part of. And they became inspired.

What this example illustrates is how those who follow an entrepreneur will also follow suit. If the entrepreneur is complacent, others will be, too. If the entrepreneur allows a vision everyone likes to shine, others will take part and shine, too. This mentality will apply to customers as well as employees. If they are excited about your business service, they tell their friends. When their friends are satisfied, your original customer gets validation.

So vision is a part of the intellectual capital of your business. With it you can succeed; without it, your entrepreneur's attitude gets short-circuited. That is, you recognize opportunity but have little desire to go get it.

THE ROLE OF CREATIVITY

Creatio ex nihilo—"to create from nothing." Life is most meaningful when we are creating something. My wife, Lori, loves to cook so much she went to a cooking school and then launched a catering business in Manhattan. Today, among all the other things she does, she loves to garden and remains a fabulous cook—creative activities. I write; help businesses take their next step; develop real estate opportunities; grow roses; and work in my woodworking shop. These are creative outlets for me. Creative acts give life more meaning. What is creative about your life and your work?

Entrepreneurs have a unique chance to derive meaning and fulfillment from their career paths if they use creativity to give form to their visions. Finding opportunity, filling it, and profiting from the effort is a highly creative, and meaningful, act. Vision supported by creativity allows entrepreneurs to take command of their lives and ensure no one else fills these shoes.

Once you start creating a new perception for yourself, uncertainty starts to fade. Every minute spent thinking about what can go wrong becomes a minute spent thinking about what can go right. Your "EQ" rises and with it the power to succeed at your entrepreneurial pursuits.

Dreams beget the vision for your entrepreneurship. Vision is a characteristic that distinguishes entrepreneurs as leaders and not managers. Give your vision a voice by allowing it to lead you through the transition. As you do this you will lead others that may be associated with you, too. Your shift to entrepreneurship requires a clear vision of what it is you, the leader, plan to achieve. Once you have that, it becomes the seed of entrepreneurship that will grow to become profitable through the efforts of good management.

Money creates choice. Choice gives you freedom. Freedom is at the root of most anonymous entrepreneurs' desire to strike out on their own.

Learning to connect with your creative vision and translate it into specific action empowers your transition to entrepreneurship. This is the objective of Step 5. Once achieved, you also will be able to maintain this energetic state. If you can succeed here you will empower others to do the same—your employees or customers perhaps. The ability to recharge yourself with your own vision rolls out the yellow brick road to real freedom. Learn this step and it's yours.

THE SOURCES OF VISION We all have vision but sometimes it's just harder to see, so we apply Step 1 and start looking in different places. Carl Jung said active imagination, a form of daydreaming, is nearly as powerful as our dreams. Thus the well of your imagination might be a good place to find vision. Set up a scene and then watch it play out on your mental movie screen. Visions of new ideas are inside of you, waiting for an opening to make themselves known.

Your image of a business idea does not have to take on Steven Spielberg proportions to be valuable, however. Take a look at the infomercials on late night television to see the visions of others who are succeeding as entrepreneurs. When I sold small businesses early in my career, many people inquired about specific businesses we offered. Some tended to think there was only a certain type of business they wanted, but this wasn't true—their vision was to own a business, almost any small business, that would produce a profit. Regardless of what type of vision you have, it's important to remember where it might lay. Some call it the subconscious; others refer to the imagination; still others name the source the soul. Whatever the label, it's there ready and waiting for a stage call. When you identify a fruitful idea for entrepreneurship, the feeling often follows it was there all along. As they say, the best ideas are usually right under your nose, which can obstruct the view.

Getting a fresh perspective, looking at things from a different angle, offers a good way to begin mining for a vision. Research work or business opportunities other than the one you have in mind. Go talk to people who operate those businesses and find out what they know. Discover what gets in the way of their success, too, so you can learn from their mistakes. A vision for you will evolve.

The reward of bringing a vision to life causes many to claim they would do it again for free. How many times have you heard successful people express their disbelief that they receive pay for doing what they love to do? What they've done is no different from the transition to entrepreneurship you propose to take.

The famous Italian artist Michelangelo was asked how he released his magnificent David from a square block of marble. He answered, "I saw the completed statue inside the stone and removed the parts that weren't

SHAPING A VISION

necessary." Like Michelangelo, discovering your vision within involves removing what's covering it up. It isn't marble that stands in your way, though. It's uncertainty, complacency, and frustration. The Entrepreneur's 12-Step Program offers a set of sculpting tools to help you chip away attitudes that stand in your way. The cumulative effect of all steps leading to this one cuts away enough to see what you're driven to create.

In developing a vision your first act should be to write it down. When describing your vision, stay simple and succinct so it's easy to focus on the big picture and not get lost in the details. (You'll have plenty of details to worry about later, and they will come and go.) This vision must remain a permanent part of what you do, and everything else must become part of it. All too often we tend to allow small projects to take on greater importance than the big idea through the time we give them. That's a big mistake. Have you ever observed someone staying very busy by moving a pile—literally or figuratively—from one side of their desk to the other and then back again? It is likely she or he had no vision of the big picture. Without one this could be you.

Once the vision takes form on paper, the next step is to determine if it's feasible. Ask yourself if you have the resources to pursue it. What factors will stand in your way? You can assess the value of your vision by comparing it to others, too. For example, I had a vision of writing a book like this long before leaving my real estate executive career. But the work and environments were not compatible. I found others who had the same problems. Eventually my vision became more important, so I left to become an author, consultant, and investor. My vision no longer has me positioned at the top of a large company. I enjoy the freedom of entrepreneurship on terms compatible with my objectives.

This revisits the point that to make the transition to entrepreneurship, change is often necessary. As previously illustrated, a job can be the sacrificial lamb. Therefore, do your homework about your vision and don't kid yourself. Can it produce? If so, can it be done part-time while you keep your job? Are there ways it can be done with less money instead of more? I have invested more than I want to in computers, but I have little need for a secretary, which would be far more costly. These are the elements of shaping your vision.

Next, seek independent advice, since you'll find good entrepreneurs often have good consultants to rely on. Prepare your ego in advance, because the best consultants are most honest and get right to the point. Sometimes that's hard to take, but if you listen you can benefit. If you don't, you can fail. Are you prepared to trade an inflated ego for improved results? Or are you willing to commit a large portion of your savings—your security cushion—to support the creation of a business with a high potential for failure?

To engineer your transition to entrepreneurship, you must *really* want to try out a new idea. You must *really* need to start or run a business yourself. You must *really* believe you can succeed. You must *really* be prepared to go it alone. Rest assured, if you don't do these things to support yourself, no one else will. Don't overcomplicate the effort. Shape a vision that's based on simple realities. They're the strongest.

SHARING A VISION

The best way to get large projects underway is with the help of others. This means getting all the parties involved in the value of accomplishing the objective. They have to understand the vision and why it's important, be willing to help make it happen, and participate in the outcome. They have to take ownership and you must give it to them. Powerful stuff.

Within limits committed entrepreneurs are comfortable sharing their vision with employees, bankers, lawyers, accountants, customers, spouses, and anyone else willing to listen. Anonymous entrepreneurs often are not. It takes courage to articulate a vision because until you do nobody believes in it. In the beginning you stand alone. Also, your vision may become the measuring stick against which you'll be compared in the future. It's a commitment. I became acquainted with a successful investor years ago who told me he started telling everyone he knew his goal was to make $1 million per year. Pretty soon they all started expecting him to do it, but so did he. When we met he was making $2 million a year.

The most important person you must share your vision with is your significant other or spouse. Never underestimate the importance of their support for your vision of entrepreneurship. If you don't have it, the chances of failing are far greater than if you do. More importantly, your spouse will often have an objective point of view to offer, so take advantage of the input. It makes sense to give her or him the chance to express an opinion, just so long as you also have a chance to disagree. Many times, however, you won't.

Sometimes rejection of your vision can occur, but don't take it personally. People may like you a great deal and just not your idea. A CEO I worked for told me my first day on the job that they could hire people to do things. What the company really needed was ideas—lots of good ideas. I was happy to oblige, but learned quickly that most of them would be rejected. Be content to position yourself as an idea fountain and handle the rejection. That's better than having to depend on others for new thinking.

And finally, another reason visions are not shared is because people are afraid others will steal their ideas. This is a lame excuse. Think about it—would you rather originate ideas or depend on others to have them? Where's the most freedom found? Don't worry too much about the theft of your ideas; it still takes an entrepreneur to make them happen, plus someone that interested may become your partner or a franchisee.

Imitation is the highest form of flattery—and often a good source of allies as well.

Releasing a vision is difficult for many entrepreneurs. It is a creation from their inner sanctum of ideas, the coin of their realm. It can be hard to do but is absolutely necessary. First, because few entrepreneurs can start *and* run a business, help from others is necessary. Second, if the vision makes good sense and attracts others to get involved, it will probably have to be altered slightly to allow for their unique participation. Changes and expert fine-tuning can season and mature a vision quickly. Letting go of the original concept enough to allow others to improve it may make your opportunity even better. This is how others develop ownership to help your vision succeed. The truly successful entrepreneur is merely a leader, the one who initiates the process and offers an occasional suggestion keep others on track.

The Greek word for enthusiasm is "enthousia"—being possessed by a god. Enthusiasm is a priceless quality successful entrepreneurs share. It's a product of vision and interior inspiration and perhaps even a bit of the soul.

INSPIRATION SHARED BECOMES ENTHUSIASM

Enthusiasm can appear in many varieties. Between lovers it means one thing; between entrepreneurs and their business it has other forms. Perhaps it's the satisfaction of a profitable month. It can arrive when you witness excitement in the eyes of an employee. It might occur in the still of the night while walking through your business alone—a silent companion with a life of its own.

To nurture enthusiasm for your entrepreneurship, find that aspect of the relationship between you and your work or business ideas that bring deepest satisfaction. Convert it into an ideal of what it might be.

Share it with others. My franchise company is over 70 years old. On becoming its president and CEO, I became the reason for the existence of my predecessors. I like to think of building that company as building a vision that will continue to inspire others 50 years in the future, perhaps the grandchildren of today's employees. Their existence will be the reason for mine. Consider important aspects of your business like this when talking to others. Enthusiasm makes a business thrive.

Here's a story to conclude with that illustrates the importance of holding to a vision even when nothing seems to be happening. Bamboo, when planted, often doesn't take off for years. But the roots must still be watered and cared for anyway. Only a vision sustains the gardener. Then, perhaps in the fifth year, it suddenly shoots up very tall. Did the plant grow in one year or five? I think it took five years to happen, four just to get ready.

Vision and ideas are like bamboo. They take time to develop and grow. Vision expressed as ideas does not equal the finished results. For every 10 bad ideas, you may have one good one. Of every 10 good ones, there may be just one that actually works. But that's the one that ignites the fires of your inspiration and that others might call their own, too.

Discovering and sharing a vision is the source of our inspiration as entrepreneurs. Sharing it with others converts it into enthusiasm. This uplifting experience also creates the real freedom you may be seeking.

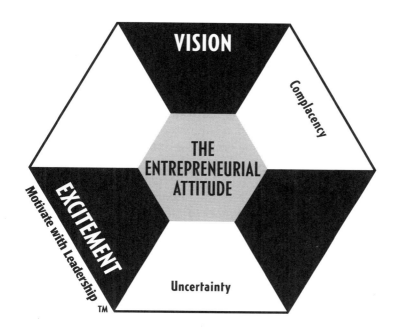

VISION

Complacency

THE
ENTREPRENEURIAL
ATTITUDE

EXCITEMENT

Motivate with Leadership ™

Uncertainty

6. MOTIVATE WITH LEADERSHIP

Strong leadership creates excitement. Imagine playing on the same basketball team with Michael Jordan. The energy we feel in the presence of highly successful entrepreneurs is palpable. Being "together" with them builds confidence and becomes an empowering experience. They are the "go to" people, because in a tough spot they know what to do and they take action; that's why they're leaders. Four ingredients—teams, perspective, respect not rank, and communication—allow them to take the lead. **Entrepreneurs teach and do.**

Whether the objective is to build a proprietorship of one or a corporation of thousands, leadership is important. Size is not the issue, teamwork is—and without it entrepreneurs will have a hard time build- **TEAMS** ing a business at all, not to mention something involving more than one person. Leaders exist because teams exist, and leadership skills form a key piece of the entrepreneur's attitude. These skills will enable you to assemble and motivate a team of employees to produce a desired result. Even if you're an entrepreneur with a single employee—yourself—leadership is the tool you will use to guide yourself and attract others as needed Step 6 of the Entrepreneur's 12-Step Program emphasizes the importance of leadership in any business of any size—they don't succeed very well without it.

Outsourcing, a popular and practical option for many businesses, gives entrepreneurs of "one" the capabilities of larger competitors. View your banker, accountant, lawyer, advertising representative, insurance agent, and most of all your customers as your team. Offer them leadership as it pertains to your objectives. Help them get excited about what you do. Unify them in your purpose and they will enjoy their participation.

Entrepreneurs often emerge naturally as leaders in a business during start-up or when they take ownership. Leadership is a job classification, however, distinct from all others. Clearly understanding this is the first step to becoming a leader.

PERSPECTIVE A leader maintains a broad perspective, focusing on the big picture while keeping in touch with the day-to-day realities of business operation. A 360-degree perspective—quite a powerful asset and the result of an open mind—can uncover unique alternatives to improve business performance. Communicating directions is the specific guidance leadership can help you provide.

To be a good leader, be willing to participate directly in any job in the business if necessary. This doesn't mean regularly do them all—just be ready and willing to answer the call. Doing so demonstrates your commitment to the overall objective and creates a sense of equality, making employees feel their job is important and they're appreciated for what they do.

Rank is not given—it is earned. Only you can appoint **RANK** yourself to the position of entrepreneur, and until you're ready to do that you will remain anonymous. Thereafter members of a team assisting you will follow your words and deeds, not your title. When you make this appointment yourself, rank evaporates, quickly displaced by respect. Then you don't need rank.

Effective leaders are quietly secure, unconcerned with bolstering their authority. What it took to earn them their place won't be erased by a challenge from another. Moreover, wise entrepreneurs will try to hire people with skills superior to their own. They surround themselves with powerful people.

Leaders who do not communicate may unintentional- **COMMUNICATION** ly encourage suspicion and a lack of confidence. Effective leaders communicate and interact frequently with employees and other team members at all levels. The absence of rank and its trappings creates a more open atmosphere where communication and performance will improve. Here's an example.

When I was a national sales manager responsible for guiding six division vice presidents, I planned an annual retreat with them that differed significantly from those held in the past. First, there was no advance agenda. The group was free to create its own on the first day. Within this framework the participants also were responsible for developing solutions over the next three days for problems they brought up.

The second difference in this corporate retreat was even though my company had four operating partners, only I attended. The participants were willing to speak candidly in this format, not telling me what they wanted me to think but what they really thought, without fear of retribution. I kept my mouth shut and learned a lot. We developed a stronger relationship based on trust, enabling us to solve many problems in the path of progress.

Leaders get better results by communicating with the business team in a structured fashion, too. Reporting general information about how the business is doing directly to employees during a meeting is one way. Don't tell them "everything," though, because it might cause them all to start looking for other jobs. That's when the entrepreneur/leader stands most alone.

When times are lean, your employees will want reassurance, so remind them of the good things in addition to the challenges ahead. Discuss concerns in greater detail with your confidants or perhaps an advisory group during a casual breakfast, lunch, or dinner meeting. In either case you have a good opportunity to discover new solutions to problems. This type of communication builds trust and respect, which again eliminates the need for rank. Plus, it is a better alternative to saying nothing, for that only allows imaginations to take over, making people think matters are better or worse than they are.

"A company takes on the characteristics of its leader."
RICHARD THOMPSON

Without a team, perspective, respect not rank, and good communication, your group has no way to measure the value of their contribution to your enterprise. In the absence of that they'll become complacent. A business does not run well without recognition of good ideas as well as half-hearted performance. Leadership creates excitement to keep the entrepreneur's attitude model from short-circuiting.

Having discussed at some length how leaders act, it's appropriate to plunge a little deeper to see what they're made of. The mantle of "leader" and "entrepreneur" is almost interchangeable. The key difference lies in that entrepreneurs are often also business owners and learn by leading themselves. You can improve your leadership skills and develop a personal vision of what a good leadership is, and then become it. As you do this, your business becomes imprinted with these qualities. You will also attract like-minded team members to assist you. This also brings added meaning to knowing and developing the positive qualities of leadership in you, descriptions of which follow.

We recruit and hire in our own image.

Teaching is as simple as show and tell. Entrepreneurs understand this because, as a practical matter, they do it all the time. Teaching is important to entrepreneurship—if you don't show others how to do what you've been doing, you'll never have time to do anything else. So you won't be able to grow by adding new activity. To teach effectively you face three important considerations.

"LEADERS TEACH"

First, the teaching environment should be friendly, even fun. Recall brainstorming sessions you've sat in on and how unusual the activity can become. The intent is often to make people laugh and loosen up. Happy people think better, learn more at a faster rate, and retain information longer. We remember pleasant experiences.

Second, the information you present should be relevant. People don't make a living with theories alone. Get to the point, make the point, and emphasize the reason for the point. Intelligent adults are smart enough to pick up information they can use on their own. They don't need motivational speeches—they seek empowerment through an expansion of their abilities. Then they'll still be excited six months later.

Third, because we learn by doing, leaders as teachers find ways employees can use new information immediately. That imprints the value of the information in their minds. The most successful entrepreneurs teach themselves as they teach others. Try occasionally asking team members to lead a discussion on something they know nothing about and they will learn about it quickly.

In my franchise company we built a one-week training program called UNITEDPOWER!™. Its components included a conspicuous absence of motivational speeches; extensive information that served a variety of uses; lots of exchange between participants; and an emphasis on having lots of fun. Many highly experienced franchisees came and learned more than they expected time after time. Some even returned for a second session. As a result this became the most successful training program in the company's 70-year history.

Eventually, you will teach the Entrepreneur's 12-Step Program to others who will wonder how you built and maintain your powerful entrepreneurial attitude. This act confirms you have one.

"CENTERED" Leaders become centered in their business by positioning themselves as a nexus—a link between several points of reference. From here they stay familiar with all points of view and manage information like it's money. They direct it to places where it will improve what works and eliminate what doesn't. This enables leaders to respond quickly, a key competitive tactic over larger, slower competitors, and learn new tactics rapidly so they can teach other team members.

First-time entrepreneurs taking on an existing business or a franchise learn by looking for information the prior owner or franchise trainers suggest to them. Useful input can be as simple as sales versus expenses for the week. Or it can be a more complicated combination of activity reports that describe sales, production, and cash flow, and trend analysis. The complexity can continue infinitely. Observing these data over time allows you to notice how they fluctuate with changes in your strategies, seasons, or competitive advances.

Very importantly, when performance is poor these advisors often have the benefit of knowing what business strategies have worked previously. Practice imitative entrepreneurship.

If, on the other hand, you're starting a business from scratch, becoming an information nexus begins by learning how to measure business performance. Then you have to learn what to do to improve it. You can probably do it all, but can you before your investment resources run dry? That's where an owner's advisory board can be so helpful. Members help you learn how to analyze your business and recommend basic strategies to improve. Plus their advice is often a fraction of others available elsewhere.

Never underestimate the number of entrepreneurs who fail without ever knowing why. That's because they didn't become an information center in their own business. Fortunately, there's an easy way to prevent this: find the problems and fix them. Take this approach and you'll have all the information you need, front and center.

"DELEGATE"

Leaders delegate because they recognize employees have a desire to do a good job—and not because they have too much work to do. Delegation should begin with the recognition that team members want to spread their wings and see what they can accomplish just like leaders once did. When team members learn to "fly," they're empowered and will want to do more. Can you guess whom they often carry? Leaders who recognize growing pains in others delegate unselfishly. That helps build more leaders, which is a source of intellectual capital in a business.

Delegation can have a negative side, too. Not all employees are made of leadership timber. Some are routine oriented and have reached their level of comfort. Don't discount such people because they want no additional responsibility—they have their place in business and should be respected for knowing their limit. In fact, sometimes they know their limits better than we entrepreneurs know ours.

Employees will always appreciate the leader who gave them an opportunity to grow. Recipients of this type of trust usually return it in equal proportion. They also know where to go to find additional opportunity—you. The relationship expands, grows, and becomes more meaningful when you delegate exciting opportunities you love.

Here's an illustration. I expanded media relations in my company and invited one of the division vice presidents to join me for an interview with CNN. His excitement was obvious when we entered the atrium at the Omni in Atlanta. The look on his face when he saw those huge CNN letters on the wall showed me the power of delegation. This is another power tool.

Keep in mind when you delegate to another he or she may perform differently than you. Observe carefully and practice restraint! Sometimes they get better results that way—hopefully better than you did. Proper use of delegation creates synergy. Leaders instinctively know it builds esprit d'corps, empowering a team and igniting business performance.

"STRONG, NOT TOUGH" Someone I respect once told me, "Understand that you're usually on the wrong side of the river. The growth and profit you want is on the other side, and to get from here to there you have to build a bridge. Some of your team get to walk across that bridge; others get to be the bridge." Good leaders are strong enough to tell it like it is. Weak leaders are tough, often hiding the truth, and never last. Strong ones do.

Strong leaders are candid and sometimes uncomfortably honest. More often than not they use diplomacy to get their point across, but not always if they want to grab your attention. If they're good, feelings don't affect their opinions; only results do. So, if we examine their candor, we see it's really offered to get to the point quickly, saving time and promoting progress.

Tough leaders are usually noisy and frequently difficult because they're unsure of their responsibility and authority. Viewing others' quest for growth as a challenge to their authority causes conflict. Leading by intimidation is no more than a simple-minded effort to draw on rank instead of logic and keep authority intact. Tough leaders are occupied with short-term issues at the expense of long-term results. They focus on what's good for them, and as a result team members eventually look elsewhere for opportunity.

Strong leaders focus on what is good for the company before thinking of themselves. In fact, "Company first" is their motto. If you don't prioritize the company in all decisions, it will not—cannot—perform to its potential. When this happens, maximum benefits for customers, clients, or employees along with the entrepreneur's success are limited artificially. Leaders take full responsibility for pushing their vision from the concept formation stage into a performing reality. They lead the way to their objective.

Strong leaders are disciplined. As negotiators they identify the core of an issue to form balanced opinions. They take a stance, stick to it, and get what they want because it is what they need—or walk away. They never bluff. Strength of character accompanies them through challenging situations, keeping them on point toward the goal. They avoid excuses and accept the buck when it stops at their desk. As a result, strong leaders have resolve that shows up as a quiet determination to succeed. This provides a measure of comfort to employees who want to follow a steady hand at the helm.

"PRINCIPLED" Principles render leaders powerful and illustrate the rules of the game to others. In business such beliefs are often shared in the form of a mission statement. Principles are easy to talk about but often hard to practice because they can create conflict between *wants* and *needs.* However, this is the stuff long-term results are made of and it helps the team know what they can count on. Say what you mean and mean what you say.

Providing good leadership involves identifying principles to set the pace and tone of activity in a company. For example, accountability from all persons without exception is one of my principles. As a result, employees view leadership as fair and trustworthy. They may not like it, but they'll respect it. Given the choice, entrepreneurs will favor respect over admiration.

It's the entrepreneur's job to define principles and demonstrate a commitment to them via performance. These standards should be consulted and maintained in the face of challenges from short-term conflict. I have seen many occasions where it would be convenient, and certainly more popular, to modify a principle over an issue. When people threaten to quit and do damage to a company thereafter, the temptation to give in can be great. During these times leaders can capture the greatest respect from other teammates by holding firm, and they'll win in the long term. When you capitulate under pressure, the outcome is sure to be another challenge followed by more. Eventually your principles become eroded completely, and nobody wants to be part of a business that doesn't stand for anything.

"ANALYTICAL" Leaders need analytical skill to balance their judgment in all the decisions they have to make. It helps measure the effects of their choices, too. Many times leaders must respond quickly, and flawed decisions risk increasing costs and reducing quality. They also pack a wallop to your bottom line.

My first lesson in business analysis came in my mid-twenties. Upon my promotion to manager of a jewelry store, the owner told me this: "Money comes in as sales, which you put in one pocket. You pay bills and what's left goes in the other pocket until I ask you for it. How much you have to give me determines your bonus." I still use this advice today despite how much more complicated business has become.

All the levers that you can move to create change produce a different result. Good leaders must know when to use any one or a combination of these devices to produce favorable results. You can only do this by learning to size up situations fast, developing the ability to measure the impact of your options. These analytical skills include familiarity with business operations, resources, and profit; without them comes less ability to determine appropriate responses and instill confidence in your leadership.

"CONSENSUS BUILDERS" Good leaders seek the opinion of others before making certain decisions. One such method, leading by consensus, involves gathering opinions from key players to make a decision representing the general thinking of the group. This strategy offers an effective way to encourage greater ownership of and commitment to final decisions. These are still made by the entrepreneur, as he or she has the last word.

Leadership by committee is different. There is a saying that goes "Committees are groups that keep minutes and lose hours." Unfortunately this is true more often than not. Typically members of a committee talk about a decision, sometimes even vote on one, but the work often ends there. For some reason they don't do anything about it, and that's how things don't get done. The individual members must not mistake participation on a committee for execution of their actual responsibilities. Essential skills needed to practice consensus building include communication, meeting management, and comfort with authority.

Selection of the key players to build a consensus group is the first step in attempting this management style. Examine the chemistry among prospective members. Average hard-working people who get along well can do more than a bunch of highly talented prima donnas who all want to shine as individuals. Good choices might include a well-informed representative from each key area of your business. Or, if you're a business of one, network with people who have similar challenges.

In the case of a business with 10 employees or less, form an owner's advisory group to meet monthly and review your progress and help improve results. It might include three or four business people you respect. If you have a larger company, a CEO advisory board can help guide you along as well. Look to the experience of retiring executives and don't underestimate their talent, drive, or ambition. The ring of the bell still makes them want to run . . . many times rings around you because they've already been where you are going.

A thorough description of any issue under consideration should be distributed to each member of a consensus group. The meeting is to discuss different points of view and their impact on company results, and then to reach a decision. It's not a school for members who won't take the initiative to familiarize themselves with the issues beforehand. Circulate the agenda in advance, too. Consensus builders do not deliver surprises at a meeting when others have not had a chance to prepare.

Effective leaders ensure a consensus meeting starts on time. Extraneous discussion is limited. All participants have plenty of time to express themselves so long as their remarks are not redundant; as a result, the conclusion being sought will emerge during the final part of the meeting. (Thus, keep an open mind throughout the process.) Once all opinions are received and discussion offers nothing else new, the skilled leader interprets and fashions opinions into an overall viewpoint. This is the prevailing belief or consensus of opinion.

Consensus building is a valuable leadership strategy because all team members involved get to have a say and create a stake in the final decisions, which encourages long-term support and performance. The work environment is more open and receptive to ideas that create opportunities. This is a participatory style of leadership that excites employees.

"DECISIVE"

Leadership and entrepreneurship don't constitute a popularity contest. You can't please all the people all the time. I once hired a new employee who got so mad at me on her second day she nearly quit. The personality clash created then was never fully resolved, but she performed well and showed initiative, which was enough for me. From time to time I requested reports from this employee as well as others. In each case I made it a point to offer my comments in writing within 24 hours. Despite our difficult relationship, this employee told me she appreciated my prompt attention and decisiveness. It gave her necessary direction and showed I cared about her and her work.

Being decisive is one of the most important leadership attributes an entrepreneur can offer. It lets your team members confidently focus on their contribution to your business. Indecision sends the signal employee concerns are unimportant and not worth the effort. Team members follow your example and respond in kind.

"PERSISTENT"

When I used to train real estate agents, I asked them how long they would pursue this difficult career choice before giving up. It was a test to reveal their persistence. If they answered by offering any amount of time, six months or a year or whatever, this usually became a self-fulfilling prophecy.

Entrepreneurs are salespeople who know it takes time to develop a business. They also know it's not uncommon to be turned down several times before the sale is made, but most will stop their pursuit after being rejected only once or twice. As a result the 80/20 rule applies—80 percent of the sales are made by 20 percent of the salespeople. The 20 percent I'm talking about are the leaders, those who switch tactics and keep pursuing the sale after all others have quit.

Persistence prevails while others fail.

When you're starting a new business, buying one, or launching a part-time entrepreneurial opportunity, you will find plenty of reasons to quit and plenty of people to tell you that you cannot succeed. Persistence is a major way you demonstrate your belief and encourage your own success. There's no question most of my success is more a result of persistence than something I do better than all others. I know, as do other entrepreneurs, you ultimately lose only when you quit.

Still, the absence of acceptable results in the face of continued effort can be frustrating. Unfortunately, many give up the goal when they should have given up one tactic for another. This is another reason why a broad perspective is so valuable to a leader. This tool brings more options into view, and for an entrepreneur it's options that keep you moving forward.

Stories of easy success tell only 10 percent of the truth. Like an iceberg, success requires 90 percent of something you don't see from the surface. Getting through all that takes persistence. How much is a relative question, which everyone needs to measure for him- or herself. Keep in mind, however, that Colonel Sanders's attempts to sell his chicken recipe were rejected over 70 times. Be persistent.

Barnyard wisdom says you catch more flies with sugar than salt. Effective leaders do not create captives out of employees; they strive to captivate creative people. And generosity with your time, spirit, and money gets this job done well. This attribute draws the line in the sand between entrepreneurs who will make it to the top and those who get stuck on a lower rung.

"GENEROUS"

Leadership must reward employees, and recognition can come in the form of money, responsibility, and assorted other benefits. But how much is enough? There are often two prevailing opinions on this issue. One is to base pay on what the company can afford without regard to the external environment. Typically this leads to offering as little as possible for as much as can be received. This strategy is costly, often leading to poor results.

Internally oriented compensation plans seem to encourage employees to survey the market for better opportunities. If they find them, they leave. More employees have to be hired to replace them. Below-market wages don't attract the "cream of the crop" and thus output capacity is limited. Moreover, new employees must be trained, requiring the time and attention of other employees. In the final analysis, no excitement is generated and results suffer.

An alternative approach to compensation is a more generous one. Consider this. Once, as I choked over the proposed cost of an advertising campaign, the agency representative said smoothly, "What does the cost matter if the program gets the results you want?" He had a point there.

Rewarding employees generously helps you do a better job of getting what you want. Effective leadership surveys the market and keeps compensation and benefits ahead of the trends wherever possible. This helps build intellectual capital in a staff that's capable of superior performance. The additional cost is less than the price of frequently hiring and training new employees and coping with production slowdowns in the meantime. Employees and customers treated like kings and queens have better attitudes, too. If they're properly motivated, with generosity directly tied to results-related activity, peak performance is encouraged. Both become golden gloves, making it difficult to leave for another opportunity. This is how leadership can create excitement.

Leaders must also be generous with their time and observations. It's easy to reward the big things that people do. But rewarding the small successes is just as important, even though there's a tendency to think they don't matter as much. Actually, sometimes they matter more. Recognizing the small things says you have made an extra effort to praise the extra effort made. A pat on the back, a compliment, or handwritten note thanking a team member for a job well done adds more to the compensation package than you can imagine.

"PRIZE LOYALTY" Recently I overheard an elderly man speaking of his wife to whom he had been married for 50 years. When asked about her health, he indicated it was declining a bit but said this was no problem. He explained that when he returned from World War II he was pretty banged up, and she had helped him recover over several years. Now "it was only right" that he did the same for her. She established a standard for loyalty in their marriage then that five decades had not diminished.

Leaders can learn much from this example as they see the sad evidence of a "me-now" mentality all around them. There's no place for loyalty to flourish when emphasis rests on short-term goals and not long-term objectives. Without loyal owners and employees, work becomes a "what have you done for me lately" place. Loyalty may seem less common but it's no less valuable today as a principle of business leadership.

Successful entrepreneurs will start the loyalty cycle by putting their best foot forward first—then they expect loyalty in return. Loyal employees work harder, have more ideas, and stay with a company longer. Loyalty creates excitement and an association that is professional and profound. When the objectives are correct and the sense of honor high, loyalty—and increased profits—are your prize.

Dance with them that brung you.

These are the traits of leadership. We share them with others by developing them in ourselves. In this way employees witness what works for us and emulate that behavior. When these new skills work, employees get excited about their new capabilities. Truly, leadership by example is the most powerful way to link opportunity to dependable, rock solid performance.

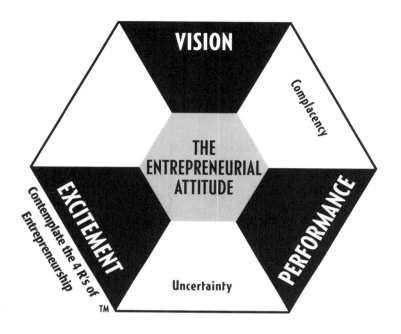

The diagram shows a hexagon. Outer labels: VISION (top), Complacency (upper right), PERFORMANCE (lower right), Uncertainty (bottom), EXCITEMENT (lower left), Contemplate the 4 R's of Entrepreneurship ™ (left). Center hexagon: THE ENTREPRENEURIAL ATTITUDE.

7. CONTEMPLATE THE 4 R'S OF ENTREPRENEURSHIP

Be present— observe. For entrepreneurs learning is a life-long activity that has no end. Their business is a center of education, replacing schools of younger days. The challenges of ownership are opportunities to expand knowledge. Progress is measured by business performance compared to plan. Consequences are greater. Poor results create a setback. Favorable results signal that advancement to a higher class may occur. The only difference in the comparison between a business and school is graduation; for entrepreneurs, there isn't any.

Learning is also a two-way street. Have you ever noticed when talking with some people it feels like they're somewhere else and haven't heard a word you've said? They don't make much eye contact and seem completely detached. This is worse than not listening—it's not even being there *to* listen.

Those truly present look you in the eye and connect with you and your message. They lock onto its content and don't think about what they're going to say next while you are talking. They focus on the substance of the exchange. Being present and observing, such as described, makes a smart listener as well as a good one. When you're a good listener, you get to add what someone else knows to your own reserves. You grow. When you're not present and observing, you're not growing. "Being there" sets the stage for contemplating the 4 R's of entrepreneurship: reward, reputation, resources, and risk.

Just how lucrative can a career in entrepreneurship **REWARD** become? Wealth-building opportunities such as those illustrated on the following page in "Earning Potential for the Small Business Entrepreneur" crop up every day for entrepreneurs committed to business ownership as a long-term play. But there are other rewards in addition to money—the confidence you can create success without depending on anyone else, the financial autonomy, creative fulfillment, and so forth. A balanced entrepreneurial attitude goes hand in hand with these results.

Frequently, though, entrepreneurs become so enamored with the excitement of the pursuit they forget why it's important. Though constantly in motion, they never make progress. These would-be success stories can find themselves facing never-ending challenges without ever landing on the promised payday.

Other times entrepreneurs get so taken with the promise of financial success, they forget to maintain the quality of life that leads to the doorstep of opportunity. Keeping a balance prevents estrangement from children, divorce, and the long-term physical effects

EARNING POTENTIAL FOR THE SMALL BUSINESS ENTREPRENEUR

Consider the following scenario. You build or acquire a small business worth $100,000 using a $25,000 down payment and finance the balance for five years. The business pays for itself during that time and appreciates at a modest rate of 1 percent annually. After the fifth year of ownership, you sell and reinvest an estimated 70 percent of the sales price (after tax proceeds) as a 25 percent down payment on the next business you buy under the same conditions as before.

Initial Investment	New Business Price	Sales Proceeds Before Taxes	Cash to Pocket or Reinvest
$25,000	$100,000	$105,101	**$73,571**
$73,571	$294,283	$309,294	**$216,506**
$216,506	$866,024	$910,200	**$637,140**
$637,140	$2,548,559	$2,678,561	**$1,874,993**

You retire with close to $2 million after 20 years. This does not include all you have earned and accumulated through savings along the way, which can be substantial.

of stress. Not to mention the expense of all the above. These costs—emotional and financial—diminish the value of sought-after rewards.

Contemplate carefully what it is you want from your entrepreneurship. It's not a get-rich-quick scheme; it's a long-term plan, deserving of serious consideration. Pay attention to what you ask for. You will very often get it.

REPUTATION I once hired a talented public relations officer. While in New York conducting a media tour, we were walking down Park Avenue toward Grand Central Station. This is Mecca for entrepreneurs. I asked my associate why he went to work for me when other opportunities were available. He answered by telling me I had a reputation for performance. After observing me for more than a year, he confirmed to himself I did everything

I said I would do. This is an example of how a good reputation opens doors of opportunity. **With a good reputation, you have the ability to attract others.**

Being an anonymous entrepreneur may mean you don't have much money to launch your first pursuit. You may need partners to get started. For this reason your reputation is among the most valuable resources you have.

Protect your reputation by making thoughtful, careful choices about those you associate with. What type of reputation do they have? If it's not consistent with your values, you may become tarnished by association.

Pay attention to what *you* do, too. Avoid excessive focus on short-term solutions, for example, because short-term thinkers often have a credibility gap that prevents them from attracting long-term players interested in lasting opportunity. And don't be afraid to hold fast to an ethical solution, even if it seems costly to do so. You may not have as much to jingle in your pocket for awhile, but your self-respect will profit enormously. Besides, the financial rewards will follow, and when they do you'll enjoy them more.

Build a quality reputation by setting a good example others can follow. In many circles it's acceptable to engage in lesser behaviors because everyone else does it. That's not good enough. You can develop a better reputation by rising to a higher standard of performance. Others will notice, and your reputation will bring you leadership opportunities.

Financial success is a primary component of your entrepreneurial objectives. When you achieve it, you can be proud. If you build a quality reputation for yourself along the way, you can be whole.

RESOURCES

There are six resources in your business that contribute to profitability: finance, control, marketing, sales, production, and service. Become acquainted with each of them independently and as they work together to ensure you maximize results.

"Rule Number One: Never run out of cash. Rule Number Two: Never, ever, run out of cash." PROFESSOR FRAN JABARA

Finance & Control. In many ways, finance and control are the recognition factors in any small business you create. These elements reflect leadership's ability to find opportunity and execute appropriate strategies, converting the mix into a profitable enterprise. Finance is your ability to manage your cash, which sets limits on what you can and cannot afford to do. When you know these things, you have control.

When you're out of cash, it becomes very difficult to find and execute alternatives to tactics that haven't worked. As a result, you are limited to those few options that don't use cash. Further, when you run low on cash, the cost of acquiring more is high. It takes time to secure financing, which could allow a window of opportunity to close. Plus, financing to replenish cash reserves adds interest costs, increasing your business overhead.

To further emphasize the importance of conserving cash, imagine the story of a farmer who desperately needed to borrow some money. He went to the local banker with his loan request for $5,000. The banker refused, saying he already held everything the farmer owned as collateral for his other loans. The farmer persisted until finally the banker made him an offer. He said, "One of my eyes is glass. If you can tell which one it is, I will give you the loan." The farmer looked him in the eyes and quickly chose the left one. The banker was surprised at how quickly the farmer made the correct choice and asked him how he figured it out. The farmer replied, "I detected a hint of sympathy in that one."

Your banker is your ally, so treat him or her like one. By all means consider leverage and financing for major purchases. But, remember too your banker is a businessperson and will expect to make a profit if you need financing because you ran out of operating capital. If you don't keep cash on hand, you may be forced to pay.

Low cash reserves affect your business in other ways, too. Employees can smell instability and morale starts to decline. Suspicious suppliers cancel favorable credit terms. Competition can take advantage of your weakened state, impacting customer loyalty.

Maintaining a capital base ensures you can sustain momentum that was costly to create. But as true and serious as all this is, here's the reality for most entrepreneurs: You may never have enough cash in your business. And if you ever do, it probably means you're not growing. That's because if you have a surplus of cash, it should be reinvested into more inventory, new services, additional marketing, repayment of debt, and so forth. The secret to learning finance and control is balance.

Finance and control form the brains of a business, the center where opportunity is recognized. The entrepreneur's goal is to create more profit in a budding business by spotting and preventing obstacles from developing before they start. When this gets overlooked, too many obstacles throw finance and control in a state of crisis management. Short-term thinking prevails. The business suffers at the mercy of the market and other competitors.

Rule Number 2 is as simple as the first: "You only improve profit by reducing expenses and increasing revenue." Cutting expenses is, as you have already read, the equivalent of eliminating waste. It's easy to imagine how less waste can favorably affect business results. Cutting expenses, as a primary management tactic, is a limited way to build financial results, though. It is finite.

Increasing revenue is the more creative way to build a business. This involves recognition of opportunity, excitement to motivate a team, and performance to capitalize on the opportunity. Increasing revenue offers an infinite source of new capital.

Rule Number 3: "Don't mix income streams." A variable income with fixed expenses can evolve into a high mortality rate. That's one reason four out of five real estate agents fail in their first five years. When the revenue flows, they get rich because overhead does not increase proportionately. But when the revenue falls, they wash out fast because the overhead remains.

When you plan your business, attempt to match fixed expenses with fixed income and variable expenses with variable income. Your chances of success will be greater for having made the effort.

Marketing & Sales. Two elements forge the emotional content of a business—marketing creates excitement, and sales take advantage of it. Without marketing to position your business, it can't get recognized. The neon arrow of marketing also shows the world how your company is different from all others. When you do this plus take advantage of the attention created to improve sales, this aspect of your business is performing correctly. When any or all of this does not happen, poor sales and declining employee morale set in.

The key thing to remember about marketing is what it is: *how your business communicates to your customers.* Make it attractive and directed at your target market. Emphasize the benefits you offer as well as the customer's need. Increase consumers' perception of your product's/service's value. Do these things well and you will attract sales.

Good marketing is good salesmanship—one is the natural result of the other. Entrepreneurs must sell by conveying the value of their product or service to others. Obviously customers must have an interest, but bankers, investors, other entrepreneurs, or joint-venture partners will need convincing, too. Convincing

AN ENTREPRENEUR'S SALES CODE

- Represent your product and service accurately.

- Don't mislead customers.

- Support your statements, oral or written, with facts.

- Be courteous in the face of discourtesy.

- Success comes from out-thinking, not out-talking, your customers.

- Say nothing when you have nothing to say. Keep saying nothing when the customer has something to say.

- Good listeners make more sales than good talkers.

- You can't buy confidence and respect with profanity and vulgarity.

- Never mind the business outlook. Be on the outlook for business.

- Forget the competition. You are the competition.

- Confidence is the backbone of entrepreneurship.

- You are not dressed for work until you put on a smile.

Adapted from "The United Way — A Manual of Helpful Suggestions" by Roscoe L. Chamberlain, Founder, United Farm Agency.

selling is not complicated. I know of no better guidelines to follow than the simple set depicted in "An Entrepreneur's Sales Code."

Production & Service. In his book *Managing,* author Harold Geneen (former CEO of ITT) says performance is the only thing that counts. And that long after we are gone, the record of what we did will be measured by how well we performed. And we either did or we didn't.

The muscle of a business's performance resides in

the production and servicing departments. This is where vision and excitement convert to reality, as products built and services delivered. Do these things well and your problems will be good ones. Fail to perform in this vital area and customer dissatisfaction will quickly close your operations.

To encourage quality and performance, I give my team members red pens carrying my signature and the quote, "Quality costs when you don't have it." I emphasize this because profit is usually the outgrowth of performance linked to obsession with quality. There is always a market for the very best. Customers want to be proud of the "deal" they got from you, which encourages repeat business. Satisfy one and she or he will tell 10 others; dissatisfy one and the news will reach 20. Focus on quality, and marketing will be free to attract the attention of new customers while sales builds on the ones you already have.

Acquiring a high standard of quality will cost more tomorrow than it does today—because the continuing cost of poor quality is always more expensive over the long term. A few more dollars on production mistakes adds up. The attitude of employees who see ownership doesn't care about poor quality takes its toll. The thrill over a low price will never leave an impression that lasts as long as the disgust over poor quality. Inferior products or service need constant advertising because you won't have repeat business. The bottom line is resources: Treat your customers like royalty, and in return they will give you their lucrative business.

RISK I'm not sure if I believe in the concept of heaven or hell. Most of the time I prefer to think the afterlife begins in a coffee shop, a nice friendly place where people meet and talk. When arriving there I imagine having an opportunity to chat with someone much smarter than me. I think he or she will ask me my opinion of how my life was lived—sort of a review.

In that place it will be easy for me to accept my mistakes because I have no regrets for the things I have done. But it will be very difficult for me to accept the things I didn't do but should have—particularly if the only reason I didn't was because I was afraid to take the risk.

> "The idea of failure never even occurred to me."
> ANTOINE TOUBIA
> Restaurateur
> Wichita, Kansas

Most people want the benefits of risk without actually taking the plunge. Entrepreneurs don't see things this way because to them not taking a risk, a calculated one, is worse. For entrepreneurs there is no failure; there's only evolution from one activity to another with improvement along the way.

Risk is the possibility that you will lose something of value, presumably because of a failure. So in addition to entertaining risk, it's wise to measure it before making a commitment. In this sense, risk is a tool you can learn to use as you manage your transition to entrepreneurship and increase your success afterward.

What often stands in the way of our ability to entertain risk is the link to failing. We forget that by taking a risk a difficult situation can improve, too. Failure, on the other hand, is only a confirmation your tactics have not produced the desired result. But failure usually isn't fatal and it isn't often final. In fact, failure often reveals the secret of success. "Anonymous entrepreneurs," for example, are so named because they don't have what they want—success in business. Recognizing this condition is the key to changing it, to building an entrepreneurial attitude and incorporating successful behaviors that together lead to success.

Failure is an opportunity to eliminate one more thing that doesn't work. You are that much closer to what will work.

Failure is an opportunity to learn from the mistakes of the past and improve on the prospects of success for the future.

Failure is a chance to put an end to what isn't working, to change tactics and exercise another option. As they say, when a door closes a window always opens somewhere else.

Do not be intimidated by the failure often associated with risk. Calculate the odds, and if they look good, this is an opportunity to overcome the forces of failure. The first is fear.

Forces of Failure—Fear. Dr. Warren Molton tells a good story to illustrate the power of fear. "Death goes to town one day and Conscience meets him at the gates to the city. Conscience says, 'What are you doing here, Death?' And Death replies, 'I came to kill 25,000 people.'"

"Upon Death's departure from the city, Conscience sees it again and says, 'Wait a minute. You said you were going to kill 25,000 people. But you killed 50,000 instead,' to which Death responded, 'No, I killed 25,000 people. Fear killed the rest.'"

Fear can prove the undoing of your transition to entrepreneurship and this career choice in general. In business, failure often occurs as a cascade of events initiated by a small problem that quickly mushrooms out of control. Suddenly the problems involve major confrontations, which many of us fear. Eliminate big problems at their roots first by attending to small problems (where fear is minimal) so they don't have a chance to grow.

Fear creates frustration in your entrepreneurial attitude and can freeze you into inaction. Successful entrepreneurs feel fear but don't let it stop them from taking action—because they know it's how to eliminate the feeling. If you hold back, a fear takes control of your situation and chokes out the desired results. Fear has no power other than what you give it, so give it *none.*

Fear of failure is common, energized by unrecognized alternatives, complacency, frustrated effort, or a combination of all of these. This type of fear is very powerful. Indeed, many anonymous entrepreneurs believe in it so completely they unconsciously set themselves up for failure. But suppose they were to shake this attitude and focus instead on converting fear of failure into an expectation of success. Imagine the possibilities.

Fear evaporates when you take action.

On the flipside, fear of success is also common. Anonymous entrepreneurs with this state of mind are afraid of the responsibility and accountability that goes with succeeding. Successful entrepreneurs want *added* responsibility; they want *more* accountability. Embracing these leads to lead to more freedom to determine their destiny.

Forces of Failure—Self-Delusion. The harder you work, the luckier you get. This holds true because the marketplace is naturally positive, always looking for ways to expand. If you give it an opportunity to work its magic with what you have to offer, it just might oblige. Good times that follow can be very seductive.

When everything is going well, entrepreneurs can be tempted to believe they are the sole architects of their success. Not true. They serve as catalysts to bring teams and events together at the right time in the right place. In such exciting circumstances, an entrepreneur may start believing his or her own sweeping generalizations. Too quickly we forget the commitment of our team. What should be quiet gratitude with tones of humility can turn into arrogance. If you slip into thinking this way, disaster may be near.

Forces of Failure—Greed. Greed is financial autonomy turned into arrogance, insidiously obscuring the origins of success. If employees consciously, or even subconsciously, find you greedy or unfair, they will produce less. You should share the good fortune of your entrepreneurship and business with the business first. Replace old equipment. Expand your enterprise's capacity to perform. Remove the stress of existing debt. I know of an entrepreneur who accumulated $1 million in cash in one year from one of his businesses. He took all the money and reinvested nothing. His employees didn't like him and within two years lost what had been a profitable business.

Thus the second group to share your good fortune with is the people who worked to help you create it. Employees should get a bonus, customers a "thank you," bankers an early payoff, and investors a dividend for taking the risk. Doing this also indirectly supports the business by securing a greater commitment for the day when business won't be so good. It will come. So build your team now, because strong teams make strong businesses.

Forces of Failure—Mistakes. The arrogance created by the belief we can do it all and the greed to enrich ourselves excessively together encourage us to stretch beyond our limits. When we do this we make mistakes. Being unprepared for the challenges that will come without a sufficient cushion of resources and commitment can lead to failure.

Avoid mistakes by staying with what you know until you know something else better. Then expand. Here's a case where success can cause failure—owners who think they can expand without proper planning make mistakes. Keep your ego in check. Take your time. Make your first entrepreneurial pursuit work. Then take your time to build another. Over the next 20 years you will amass considerable success.

Managing Risk. Investing in the stock market is risky—the entire amount invested can be lost. The best way to reduce that risk is to diversify.

It is estimated that 70 percent of the risk associated with investing in stocks has to do with the companies chosen; that is, "company specific" risk. The remaining 30 percent of the risk relates to the market itself and the directions it takes. Stockbrokers reduce risk by selecting a good mixture of companies as investment positions. If one fails, the others will prevent the loss from becoming too significant. As a result of diversification, 70 percent of the risk of investing in stock can be removed.

Managing the transition to your entrepreneurship is more difficult because it will usually focus on one opportunity, and running a business thereafter is no different. In essence, we place all our eggs in one basket, losing the favorable influence of diversification. But there is a way to improve your position.

When you become an entrepreneur, you may need to answer investors' inquiries about your results. Or you may need to visit regularly with your banker. In either case you meet with them periodically to deliver a progress report. This is particularly true when results are negative—that's when they'll want to know your plan describing what you're going to do to turn things around. If you don't have one, with options, why do they need you?

Reduce the risk of entrepreneurship by keeping lots of options available all the time. With more alternatives to consider come more chances to succeed. Also, with more alternatives you have less downtime taking a new approach if the current one doesn't turn productive.

To develop a lot of options, stay well informed about your market and your business. Listen to your employees and associates. Cultivate relationships with dynamic personalities that are highly creative and pick their brains for ideas. Read the trade journals. Find out what others do to succeed and then do that or improve on it. Develop good, but brief, reports of your business, including sales and expense overviews. Where does your business come from? What attracts your customers? A diverse selection of information helps you focus on factors you can control to improve results and remove the influences that work against you.

Even business failure can be an option to consider. In fact, some entrepreneurs buy companies they know are failing. Their intent is to accelerate the failure with a liquidation sale from which they will earn a profit. Corporate raiders do the same thing when they buy poorly performing companies for less than the value of the assets. They sell off the pieces for a profit.

The path of greatest progress is typically the one of least resistance. Therefore, entrepreneurs balance and moderate risk by choosing options that create the most results, with the least commitment of resources, for the shortest time, without contradicting long-term goals. It's only when you run out of options that you really expose yourself to the downside of risk

Successful entrepreneurs use risk to prevent the frustration of poor business results. Risk drives up the price and drives off competition. That leads to improved earnings and the opportunity for a greater marketshare.

Growing up I learned the three "R's" were reading, writing, and arithmetic. Today's children learn the three "R's" of reduce, reuse, and recycle. Entrepreneurship, however, has four "R's"—reward, reputation, resources, and risk. Carefully consider the rewards you expect, because you will often get what you ask for. Envision a quality reputation, because a good one opens doors to opportunity while a bad one nails them shut. Use resources wisely, because energy, time, and money come in limited supply. Entertain risk, because it can lead to disappointment or spectacular success. Contemplate these four R's wisely and they will help educate your growing entrepreneurial attitude.

"Performance overpowers frustration."

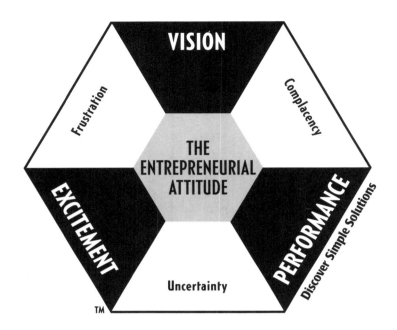

THE ENTREPRENEURIAL ATTITUDE

VISION

Frustration

Complacency

EXCITEMENT

Uncertainty

PERFORMANCE

Discover Simple Solutions

™

8. DISCOVER SIMPLE SOLUTIONS

Less is more. Early in my career as an entrepreneur I sold business opportunities. This required the ability to determine business value, a fairly specialized skill. A business owner approached me to sell his property, so I completed an evaluation. As was typical, he wanted twice as much as it was worth, so I declined to list the property.

A few months later that business sold through one of my competitors who knew little about business valuation but a lot about listing. The sales price was what I had originally calculated—but half the asking price. After expressing my frustration to my broker, he said I was probably smarter when I was dumber.

Keeping a business going can present numerous challenges. Often each day brings a new problem. In addition, since entrepreneurs have a strong interest in every aspect of business, they frequently don't delegate well either. Becoming overburdened with too many things to do compromises your ability to focus on the big picture, but that focus helps you keep things simple.

Upon reading a first draft of this book my brother said, "Hey, this tells me I don't have to have a Harvard MBA to succeed in business. A good entrepreneurial attitude might take me a long way." This is true. It is easy to think business must be complicated to be successful, which is not true. In fact, simple ideas plus entrepreneurs who can stay focused on the big picture while standing in the details often succeed best. In my case, my zeal to complicate my brokerage with impressive valuations of a business overshadowed my greater objective to build a listing inventory. It cost me several thousand dollars because I didn't keep it simple.

CORE VALUES

Occasionally we have the good fortune to associate with skilled entrepreneurs who can see right through problems. They know how to identify the gears that make a business tick, and they relate all their recommendations to these inner workings. The vital mechanisms that make a business succeed are its core values, which exist in all areas: finance, control, sales, marketing, production, and service. Often they are summarized in a general income formula that describes the nature of the business revenue stream. Here's an example.

The income formula for real estate brokerage is Listings Taken times Rate of Conversion [to sales] equals Units Sold. Units Sold times Average Sale Price equals Volume. Volume times Average Gross Commission Rate equals Commission Income. Listings, Conversion Rate, Units Sold, Average Sales Price, and Gross Commission Rate thus are the core values of the income formula. Anything you can do to improve any one of these elements will favorably affect all the others. Sometimes it takes less effort to improve one that may have the potential to achieve a greater result. But no strategy or tactic should move forward without first determining its impact on the variables in the formula. Likewise, it's easier to break the big problem of making a profit into smaller problems of improving just one of these variables. Understanding core value analysis is a neat trick to improve profitability.

Other types of core values exist in a business, too. These are tied to the creation of intellectual capital—often described as "corporate culture." If it's healthy the business is more productive and capable than if it isn't. Strong leadership, a "company first" attitude, team unity, diversity, and a commitment to quality are core-value expressions of high levels of intellectual capital. They are more difficult to measure than the previous examples because of their subjective nature. But the more your business (big or small) has of them, the more money you can make on operations or an outright sale of the business.

Knowing the ingredients of a healthy financial plan and business culture as well as how to emphasize them comprise critical elements in the creation and maintenance of business momentum. Results reported measure the entrepreneur's ability to both manage and lead in performance assignments. Every business strategy and tactic executed should take advantage of and build on core values as much as possible.

INTELLECTUAL INTEGRITY Did you hear the story about the anonymous entrepreneur who had no intellectual integrity? It seemed he frequently had a problem representing facts as they really were. But smart investors soon discovered what gave him away. He moved his lips.

Another sign of low intellectual integrity occurs

when business people consistently sell out long-term objectives to achieve short-term goals. They prefer the comfort of immediate rewards over the security of increasing wealth. While this may not be illegal, immoral, or fattening, it leads one to repeat the same act over and over. Crisis management can easily prevail.

Sometimes setting aside intellectual integrity seems to offer the best solution for short-term business results, but it rarely contributes to long-term entrepreneurial success. Intellectual integrity means your intellect connects to your integrity, and as a result your leadership stays consistent with what's best for your business. Remember—company first.

Unfortunately, when intellect separates from integrity, the performance orientation of a business changes. Strategies and tactics are designed to support individual agendas, not company profitability. Employees view this form of low intellectual integrity as a sign of weak management and start to fall "out of line" in their work. Quality declines and performance is the loser.

Emotional discomfort with difficult jobs presents another common cause of low intellectual integrity. Some executives cannot hire managers with equal or greater skill—a talented peer becomes a threat due to some form of insecurity they have. As a result, they hire less than the best person for a job and performance falters accordingly.

Many other reasons may account for a loss of intellectual integrity. In nearly all cases, however, it allows the tail to wag the dog, decreasing or entirely erasing business profits. The simple solution of maintaining intellectual integrity at all times prevents many such problems.

Another simple solution that works very well, lever- **LEVERAGE**
age is created when you use a small amount of your

resources to control other resources you do not own. It's often called "OPM," which stands for "other people's money."

In entrepreneurship, creating debt is a common form of leverage put to use. Entrepreneurs invest one dollar of their own and borrow three, thus controlling an asset four times the value of their investment. The principle works fine so long as your business creates enough cash flow to repay the debt and provide a return on your dollars invested. Unfortunately, sometimes it doesn't.

Leverage has an application to time, also. When directed to this resource, recall that entrepreneurs don't always like to delegate their work to others. But time is a key ingredient to success. If you do not use your time wisely, and delegate, you are overworked. Business performance may suffer, and thus you can't successfully make the transition to entrepreneurial success. Learning to use leverage as a tool lightens your load and provides more control over your business—just as delegation does.

A third type of leverage (actually the most common) involves economies of scale. In essence, here you develop the ability to produce and sell a product or service in such volume that customers cannot acquire what you offer for less. For example, I once spent several hundred dollars renting equipment to seed my lawn. It took me one full day of back-breaking work, too. My neighbor spent $120 to hire a lawn service to seed his yard and didn't do anything but pay the bill. He got better results, too. The lawn service used economies of scale to buy better equipment than I could rent; to buy and sell me seed cheaper than I could buy it; and to provide all the labor and do the job in less time than I could do it myself. This is a very common example of economies of scale used to create a business opportunity for an entrepreneur who likes doing yardwork.

By whatever method you discover to apply leverage, here's a very potent tactic to improve business performance. Always ask yourself "Where is the leverage I can use?" in your business ideas. When found and taken advantage of, it offers a powerful push to your entrepreneurial transition.

EXPERIENCE

The experience you need for successful entrepreneurship is usually learned on the job. This is best experience you can buy, but it's often also the most expensive. Mistakes create poor business performance and an actual loss of cash—not just lower grades.

It has been my good luck to know, observe, and work with some well-known, successful entrepreneurs. Despite the diversity of their industry choices, they maintained high standards always. They were self-starters who never, ever quit. And being good was more important to them than being big. Observing them has help me learn from their experience.

Good judgment comes from experience. Experience comes from bad judgment.

The challenge of experience for most anonymous entrepreneurs, though, is getting some. For beginning entrepreneurs this isn't always easy. Many people take a take a wait-and-see attitude with new businesses—they wait and see if they survive before doing business with them.

I painted houses for three years to earn a living while attending college. When getting started I became acquainted with the owner of a well-known painter's supply. Knowing he was connected to lots of work, I asked him to recommend me if possible. He told me I didn't have enough experience, so I asked how this was possible without getting enough work to *become* experienced. He only said, "Well, if you don't get any work, you won't get any experience." Though frustrating, he did me a big favor by telling me those who have what it takes will find a way to get the experience they need. The rest won't. Eventually I did and he recommended me, too.

This is one of the challenges of the transition to entrepreneurship. You will put yourself in a position to perform. You may not know exactly how, but by observing others more experienced you can find out. Do what you think your silent mentors would do in your circumstances. The lessons you can learn this way are valuable.

Another easy way to attract the benefits of experience quickly is by using an owner's advisory board, as noted earlier. This body offers one of the most valuable resources you can find, as there's a wealth of information among successful entrepreneurs. They've done what you may be planning to do and thus can offer solutions with the potential to improve your business more in one year than you could have done in 10. And they love the process.

A collection of hard-nosed businesspersons on your board provides the objectivity you need to stay focused on the big picture. They will have no qualms about speaking candidly and telling you how the cow ate the cabbage if you go off track. An owner's advisory board can help you identify programs and people whose intellect doesn't connect to their integrity, plus they help design tactics to confront these problems head on. Be ready. Such a board can improve your performance highlighting problems and solutions you have not seen before; your challenge then will be to decide if you agree as well as have the strength to go where they point.

When used as described, the owner's advisory board becomes your voice of experience. Collectively a good board will have over 100 years of experience working at an impressive level in business management and ownership. They probably have made (and dealt with) many of the mistakes that crouch down the way in your path. New solutions you struggle over might be routine for them. Their ability to see what lies beyond your immediate situation is their greatest asset. They understand the changes a business experiences when it grows.

Forming and working with an owner's advisory board can be a tough experience for many anonymous entrepreneurs. Take a deep breath, leave your ego at the door, and keep an open mind. You can exit with strategies that will take you to the bank.

Focus Distractions in a business present costly propositions. They divert precious time and attention from core activities. Practical improvements that might have been made get lost in the whirlpool of developing new ideas that may never pan out.

Success for you as an entrepreneur often leads to thoughts of expansion, though. Growth can be the most exciting but also the most difficult part of running your business. Success can twist into a complication, a distraction that destroys good businesses before their entrepreneurs' have a chance to reap the rewards. All for ignoring the adage to "keep it simple."

Another heady but potentially damaging distraction is an unexpected opportunity to sell your business for a profit. Smart buyers approach, dangling offers and absorbing your attention. They can be really sexy, too. All throughout your communications they may try to pick your pockets for information to use as a competitive edge. Without realizing it the siren's song of a buyer seduces you into swapping your vision of your business for theirs. In the meantime you pay less attention to moving your business ahead and more attention to moving yourself out. Momentum can decline; employee morale can take a nosedive; business results may suffer, too. If that happens the buyer's offer changes to reflect new conditions, and the price starts to go down. This can seriously weaken your market position if the sale doesn't occur.

Serious buyers for your business won't play games.

They will make something happen fast since they don't want the distraction to damage the business they want to buy. Under these rules, even the most complicated, sophisticated transactions operate with one goal in mind: keep the solutions simple.

REFLECTION Even when pressed to make simple decisions, you're smart to consider the alternatives. Because obviously you can't think of them all at once, it's wise to take a little time and reflect on a few as they have a chance to occur. Compare their impacts on your business. Discuss them thoughtfully with your mentor or advisory board.

Sleeping on a decision gives you time to go through a few scene changes in your entrepreneurial script. With each, your perspective of the decision may change. New solutions will gradually start to come into view. When you have wrestled with alternatives, you can confidently confirm or reject a decision planned. A bad deal is worse than no deal. It's as simple as that.

WASTE ELIMINATION Consider this. If your business works on a 10 percent profit margin, one dollar of waste eliminated [expenses saved] equals 10 dollars of sales created. That's because 10 percent of 10 dollars is a dollar of profit or waste. Which do you have the most direct control over today?

Even the most unprofitable businesses "on paper" can still find profit if they look in their trash cans. As a business broker I could assess the impact on gross profit of waste in restaurants by looking in their garbage. There is a tendency to overestimate the amount of food to prepare. Serving too much results in unfinished meals, and food that isn't served and can't be stored is thrown out. Either causes the food cost to rise, reducing gross profit.

Inventory is a resource often affected by waste.

THE ENTREPRENEUR'S 12-STEP PROGRAM: STEP 8 121

During World War II, America's manufacturing sector expanded rapidly to accommodate a need for massive amounts of military hardware and insufficient inventory was on hand. When the war ended, though, we had a 250-year supply on hand. Two mistakes were made; one was having too little inventory and the other was having too much.

Your business may have an inventory that can create waste problems. Perishable inventory if not sold quickly gets wasted by spoilage. Poor handling and care can destroy inventory, and becomes a problem during peak seasons. Paying for inventory is costly, especially if you buy too much, but also if you buy to little and underestimate the demand to come. All of this adds up to the potential for waste—of dollars invested in excess inventory or procurement, or those spent on marketing and advertising to attract customers who will find supplies have run out when they arrive.

Compounding, the principle that makes money grow over time, works in reverse with waste. For example, in my franchise company we printed millions of property brochures. When operating a printing facility of that size, mistakes are bound to happen. But when a mistake occurs in a print run, it's multiplied several thousand times. We examined the production processes leading to the print stage, then added sophisticated computer systems to make mistakes easier to detect and less costly to correct. These adjustments reduced waste and created improvements in productivity that were magnified many times. The solution was no more complicated than the situation demanded.

Laziness among employees presents another area where waste occurs. I don't believe we should work at full speed all the time we're at work; entrepreneurship involves balance. But some people don't pick up the pace at all. The difference in time it takes them to finish a job versus the time it takes someone working at a more reasonable speed is wasted. Apply the hourly rate to that time and waste has a value. Multiply it by 52 weeks a year and the solution, as well as the problem, is simple.

Failure to observe deadlines is another serious form of waste. When teamwork is involved, deadlines for activity to be completed are triggers to the commencement of other activity. When a deadline is missed, people and resources freeze with inaction. They are put on hold, waiting and wasting their time. Try calculating the cost of labor hours wasted by many due to one person's failure to meet a deadline.

Unfortunately many are not aware waste is occurring, or they've completely accepted the idea that the business can stand the loss. That sort of thinking is *simplistic* rather than simple. How many times have you failed to pick up a paper clip? The issue is not the value of a paper clip in the trashcan, but rather the value of the discipline to save at every opportunity. Very simple, but it really adds up over a lifetime of entrepreneurship.

EMPHASIS ON QUALITY   In the aftermath of World War II, the Japanese economy was destroyed. William Edwards Deming was the management consultant assigned by President Harry Truman to help that nation rebuild. His guiding principle was to focus on quality—and rebuild they did. Today, the Deming Prize is among the most coveted industrial awards any business in Japan can receive.

A strong emphasis on quality is supported by the simple premise that nothing is so good it cannot be improved. Nothing. Because a product, no matter how superlative, cannot keep pace with constant changes in the marketplace by standing still. Products need to be modified eventually if only to keep consistent with market tastes. Indeed, the original formula for Coca-

Cola remains the same; the label on the bottle, though, has changed many times.

Emphasizing quality in production reduces mistakes. Thus, downstream the cost of the products goes down, and the amount of gross profit goes up. We often fail to recognize the value of this principle because many mistakes seem so small. But multiply them by the thousands of times they get made and the results become significant. The simple truths are continuous improvement in production to reduce errors has a direct impact on business profitability, and quality of service is equally important; a superior product is of little value if follow-up service is poor. Remember that it costs less to keep an existing customer than it does to create a new one. Give them what they want.

Quality costs when you don't have it.

Learn to recognize the core values of your business. Keep your intellect connected powerfully to your integrity. Use leverage to your advantage. Get access to all the experience possible. Stay focused and avoid distracting influences no matter how exciting. Sleep on decisions as long as it produces new alternatives. Emphasize quality. Get to know these simple solutions and find ways to apply them to your business. Give success a chance.

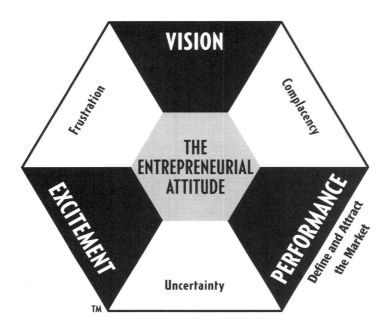

VISION

Frustration

Complacency

THE ENTREPRENEURIAL ATTITUDE

EXCITEMENT

PERFORMANCE

Define and Attract the Market

Uncertainty

™

9. DEFINE AND ATTRACT THE MARKET

To attract more customers, become more attractive. It is cheaper, faster, and easier to build your business when you can find customers who need what you offer and get them to come to you. Understanding this premise helps explain why marketing makes money.

Over the course of time many anonymous entrepreneurs have had good ideas they didn't know how to sell. As a result, the world still doesn't know what it missed. The irrefutable truth of entrepreneurship is that you need to market your products as thoroughly and aggressively as you create them. Indeed, many major corporations spend up to a third of their entire operating overhead on marketing-related activities. They know even the best product will fail without persuasive appeals to a clearly defined target market. You should know this, too.

My first serious involvement in this area came when I was asked to develop a marketing plan for a business. Though my entrepreneurial attitude was good enough to take on the assignment, my experience told me to find a consultant with the right know-how. I contacted an old acquaintance who had started and built his marketing company into a national player. What I learned from him was simple: Marketing is finding needs people have, products to fill them, and linking the two together. So, marketing is the collection of things you do to attract a target market to your product or service. This can be a complex exercise for large companies or a more simple plan suited to your transition to entrepreneurship. Both are often based on common sense.

Much of what you pay marketing experts for is to confirm, with research, what you may already know. Blue-chip companies with matching marketing budgets spend money on research to avoid spending more money on campaigns that miss the mark. The other thing you pay marketing specialists for is their ability to translate what you know into a language your customers speak. At the heart of all this, therefore, is the fact that you are usually the primary marketer of your business. Step 9 will help organize what you already know into a plan to do your own marketing, or help you know what to expect from those you hire.

Marketing is for every entrepreneur, regardless of size. In fact, it may offer the greatest potential rewards to the smallest entrepreneurs. Though it has the ability to get big results, it isn't always necessary to make a big investment in marketing. Following basic rules, you can make more progress than perhaps you'd expected.

To begin, you'll need to know 1) why anyone will want to buy what you offer (benefits); 2) who will pay for those benefits (market segmentation); 3) what themes and appeals will attract them (market differentiation or position); and 4) where you will place them to attract your buyer's attention (promotional plan). Answering these questions will protect your money and your time.

BENEFITS Recently I was approached by a service provider who wanted assistance with his business plan. Sales were not as great as expected, though his product and service were superior to all others available. More importantly, the general public would eventually have a need for what this fellow offered—but that hadn't occurred yet. It's not uncommon for anonymous entrepreneurs to be ahead of their time, and so their business launch is often premature.

In this situation the provider was attempting to sell to an as yet undeveloped need, forcing his business to accomplish two very different marketing objectives: First, create demand. Second, supply it. Few of us would have enough money to pay for the efforts necessary to create a market demand.

When buyers are aware of what they need or want, your sale is half-way made. All that remains is to demonstrate what you have by communicating your product's benefits. Examine the benefits of what you offer your marketplace. Are your product's attributes recognized and perceived as valuable? If not, even the most tasty, fat-free, no sodium, cancer-eliminating hamburger will not sell. Save yourself lots of time and money by finding something a customer base knows it wants and is willing to pay for. In this instance, as with negotiating, marketing no deal is better than pushing for a bad one.

MARKET SEGMENTATION You don't have to sell your product or service to everyone—just those within a specific target market. For example, Grape Nuts is a popular breakfast cereal in America without any direct imitators on the market.

It hasn't any grapes or nuts either, but it's remained extremely successful for years. In fact, according to an article appearing in *The Wall Street Journal* under the headline, "A CEREAL MAKER'S QUEST FOR THE NEXT GRAPE NUTS," Grape Nuts, manufactured by C.W. Post, captures 2 percent of the $8 billion annual cereal industry sales—a very impressive $160 million.

Grape Nuts is targeted at a specific segment of the total market (health-conscious people) and has succeeded in attracting it. As a result, this product is a financial success and has been in demand for over 100 years. This example and others like it provide an important clue to successful entrepreneurship: Knowing who makes up your target group is key to developing an effective marketing plan for your business.

To further illustrate the approach, consider the following. I once interviewed a potential franchisee for my real estate franchise company in Salt Lake City. He owned a metropolitan residential brokerage that sold no rural property, and his first question of me addressed what I could do to help him sell more homes in town. I told him "Nothing," and explained that my market—rural property—was just a small slice of the entire real estate marketplace. Getting as much of that as possible was all I wanted or needed. If he was interested in the same market, we should get together. This is market segmentation.

Market segmentation allows you to rule out efforts to attract buyers outside your target market area so you can sharpen your focus. Think of it as a rifle shot, where one bullet hits the bull's eye, instead of a shotgun blast, where many pellets miss the target entirely. When you employ market segmentation, your efforts take aim and thus can be more productive. You are free to develop your expertise and proficiency within a specific, narrow market range, which improves your value to customers. You can also remove distractions spurred by unrelated activity. This is important to remember for entrepreneurs— creative animals always looking for a way to stir up results. Promotional activity must be consistent with your core business focus and actually create improvements; otherwise, the cost of distractions created by building and delivering mass marketing can exceed the income it's projected to produce. Never lose sight of the market segment you serve.

MARKET DIFFERENTIATION Developing a marketing differentiation isn't rocket science. My wife had an art teacher in the eighth grade that preached to her students, "Lights on darks. Darks on lights. Contrast is dynamic. Dynamic attracts attention." The essence of communicating differentiation thus is not so complex. Identifying the dynamic in your business is the basis for developing themes and appeals that tell your market who you are. In the case of this book, notice use of the words *anonymous* and *entrepreneur* presents both ends of a spectrum. Few successful entrepreneurs are anonymous, but many who want to be successful are. Thus, a target market is defined and a theme its members can identify with appears: *The Anonymous Entrepreneur.*

Working with Step 9 employs the principle of attraction and considers how to make your business more *attractive.* One effective way is to differentiate yourself from competitors. That is, tell your customers how you're distinct from everyone else in the same game. The principle of attraction emphasizes customers' interests. Find out what will appeal to them, based on their needs, and develop short phrases or slogans that say you have it. These link a product to its customers—the primary objective of marketing.

The best themes and appeals are memorable and memorizable.

Some themes and appeals include words, others just pictures. The intention either way is to create a lasting image of your business and to increase customer's perception of your product's value. Most people believe the price of a product is determined by its cost. Not true. The price of a product is related to what people believe it is worth and what they will pay to have it. Good marketing helps consumers decide your product is worth more instead of less, which favorably affects your bottom line.

Your themes and appeals, however, are more than just slick brochures and snappy slogans. A message comes across in your logo, letterhead, and business card. In fact, the name of your company is the first and most important marketing decision you will ever make. All of these elements represent powerful first impressions. Think your messages through carefully—changing them later is more expensive than buying new stationery.

PROMOTIONAL PLAN

Besides promoting longevity, market segmentation and differentiation increase the efficiency of dollars spent on promotion. For example, advertising that describes the benefits of your product attracts more attention when placed in front of your target market. More people with a direct interest will see it. More will inquire. You'll thus have the chance to make more sales per marketing or advertising dollar invested. As a result of "targeted advertising," sales (in relation to the dollar invested) will increase, which can improve profit. This reduces the risk associated with making the decision to invest in marketing.

Building a promotional plan is challenging because many people either produce products or promote them, but seldom do both. Entrepreneurs, however, can. Clearly, an effective promotional plan includes more than a name and a sign—it conveys messages that carry the right meaning to the right market. Despite the superior effort, though, don't expect

ROYAL PROMOTION

1. GIVE YOUR CUSTOMERS WHAT THEY WANT. Replace a product orientation with emphasis on the customer's point of view. Buyers have the interest and they have the money. To attract one and earn the other, give them what they want.

2. CREATE A POSITIVE IMPACT ON THE CUSTOMER'S BOTTOM LINE. It's difficult to sell the value of benefits you offer without knowing how they will affect the customer. Whether it's a lower price or a better product, if you can't improve your customers' condition, they have no reason to do business with you.

3. DO THINGS FOR CUSTOMERS THEY CAN'T DO FOR THEMSELVES. If you provide a product or service customers can give themselves for less money or with greater ease, they don't need you.

4. IT'S EASIER TO KEEP CUSTOMERS THAN FIND NEW ONES. A dozen contacts might be necessary to find just one new customer. That takes time and money. It takes the same things to lose a customer, too. Efforts spent worrying over not servicing a customer properly and then attempting to recover are more difficult and costly than taking care of business in the first place.

5. FOCUS ON WHAT WORKS. Don't stray from what works until it stops working. Financial results will provide ample evidence. Then, find other things that do work by looking outside of the business.

6. FIND WAYS TO INCREASE MARKET SIZE. Bigger markets lead to bigger opportunity for sales and profit. Always look for ways to generate more customers for the product or service provided. This reduces incremental costs that do not have to be increased with the addition of one more sale.

7. USE THE PRINCIPLE OF ATTRACTION. Make your product or service more attractive. This brings you more business. Advertising costs will fall, and the savings can be added to the bottom line or used to create additional business.

advertising to be 100 percent effective. The famous advertising guru David Ogilvy once said, "I know half my advertising is working. I just don't know which half it is."

A common mistake for entrepreneurs occurs when money is in limited supply—the marketing budget is often the first thing cut. Keep this in mind: When you stop promoting, you stop acquiring business. When results are unfavorable for you, they may be unfavorable for all others, too. Moving counter to the direction of conventional wisdom has made fortunes. So, when others are tightening their marketing budgets, consider increasing yours. Your market share will likely expand as your competitor's shrinks. This will deliver a handsome return to your doorstep when the marketplace recovers.

To steer around another common mistake, avoid falling prey to short-term tactics that cost more to run than they produce. Sales contests offer a good example here. They must be able to generate more results than would have come in without them; otherwise, the sales incentives paid out do not produce a return on your investment. Worse, next year salespeople and customers may expect you to offer another contest that could lose more money. Find a way to make short-term sales promotions "self-liquidating," or keep your money in long-term marketing programs.

Next, promote the benefits, not the features. When you describe all the physical aspects of your product—a mistake made by earnest yet novice marketers—it has no compelling meaning or attraction for a customer. He or she wants to know what the features can do for them.

Sell the sizzle, not the steak.

For example, many real estate investors want to acquire distressed properties, fix them up, and resell them for a profit. They're not particularly interested in what's wrong with the property in the beginning, since that's expected—they just want to know if it's *distressed,* the red flag needed to capture their interest. I know a broker who found a truly distressed property and advertised it as "The filthiest place we've seen." This was a dynamic theme that held strong appeal for his target market. Many inquired.

Once you have defined the benefits of your business, a market segment, your marketing differentiation, and a promotional plan, use this hand-tailored expertise over and over, wherever and whenever possible. The continuous stream of consistent messages has a cumulative effect. Advertising a product in one big splash seldom works as well as advertising it 10 times in small placements. If you don't get sick of your themes and appeals, you aren't using them enough!

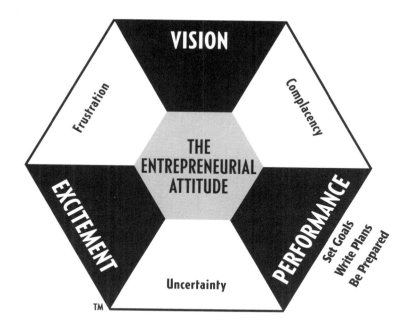

THE ENTREPRENEURIAL ATTITUDE

VISION

Frustration

Complacency

EXCITEMENT

PERFORMANCE

Set Goals
Write Plans
Be Prepared

Uncertainty

TM

10. Set Goals - Write Plans - Be Prepared

Anyone can do easy work. And if entrepreneurship was easy, everybody would be doing it, plus the rewards wouldn't be as great. But entrepreneurship offers big rewards because it involves work that is difficult to do. You can make it easier, though, by breaking difficult problems down into smaller, more manageable pieces. After being solved separately, they can be reassembled into a total solution and put to work in your business. Through all of this some people lose sight of the big picture. Step 10 is work you do to prevent this.

Regardless of business size, when you become an entrepreneur you will be accountable for the results it

Nolo supre prendre.

does or does not produce. Your responsibility extends, in varying degrees, to those who have supported you, which may include employees, suppliers, lenders, and even investors or stockholders. You'll need to communicate with them about what you are doing, and there's no better way than by having a plan.

Running a business efficiently involves maintaining a proper balance of supply and demand, support and performance, in all areas. You have to know when to step up advertising or when to buy additional inventory for Christmas; wait too long and the advertising won't work or the inventory isn't available.

Entrepreneurs constantly evaluate every aspect of their business to prevent surprises that can be costly. It's much easier to weather the tides when you have well-thought-out goals and a plan.

SET GOALS Goals are powerful binoculars that help entrepreneurs stay focused. As a benchmark of progress, they help you measure performance and stretch to reach ambitious bottom-line results. They work and make it possible for you to do the same.

Approximately 20 years ago I got involved with a goal-setting group. We met once a week and discussed ideas about goal setting. We shared with each other the goals we held individually. We learned that to make goals work, they had to be written. This was the crucial first step in goal setting.

I set goals to remodel my home. The project included central air conditioning, wall-to-wall carpeting, a new kitchen with nice appliances, and a walk-out patio. I wrote these things down, put the list in a box, and went back to work, forgetting about them entirely. A year later while cleaning out some boxes, my goal list resurfaced. To my surprise, each item had been covered. I bought a new home.

The moral of this story is "Don't worry too much

about how goals will happen." Set the goal and get back to work. We aren't smart enough to identify all the ways the future can work. It never occurred to me I would sell my house for a big profit and buy another with the improvements I was seeking. But that's what happened.

Goals should be specific, thereby improving the definition of results you hope to create. Your mind and feelings, acting together like a lens, focus energy on the creation of our vision—a composite of your goals. Thus the vision can't come true without the goals. If you find yourself living by default, just accepting whatever comes but often disappointed, now you know what's missing. To set goals and get good results, consider the following:

1. *Goals should be specific.* There was a young lady who wanted to marry a rich man. She wed a fellow with no money whose last name was Rich. Without a specific description, your goals won't happen.

2. *Goals should be written.* Capturing goals on paper makes them physical entities and therefore real. Writing them down also makes it possible to review them periodically and measure your progress. This is particularly important for entrepreneurs, who must frequently keep track of many things in a business.

Energy expended discussing a goal is the same energy that could be used to make it happen.

3. *Goals should be shared with a confidant.* This means one or a very limited number of people. Sharing goals too widely or casually often evolves into talking and not doing. In addition, talking too much about goals takes some of the edge off them. Form and keep a silent bond to achieve your goals.

4. *Goals should be realistic.* A constant diet of failure leads to personal doubt, negative thinking, and eventually self-fulfilling prophecies. This happens when goals are consistently unrealis-

tic. A common example of this is weight loss. Is the goal to lose 25 pounds or reduce weight by that much? I'm sure I lose 25 pounds a year but gain it all back and never reduce my weight. Aiming for a loss of one pound a month is realistic and has worked better.

This is not advice to settle for modest goals— just a reminder that a very high goal stays within reach if it is broken into a series of smaller, more realistic accomplishments.

5. *Goals must have a deadline.* You have to say when you're going to reach your goal. Otherwise, it could take forever, which is more time than you have.

Time management is a big issue for entrepreneurs, who all have the same amount—24 hours in each day. Its roots lie in the smallest units: minutes. Entrepreneurs who keep their goals on a timetable get the most done and obviously enjoy the most success. Billionaires cannot get anyone to pay them the hourly rate needed to reach and maintain that income level, but by managing time and confining their activities to guiding others that work for them, they do it for themselves. Those with incomes in the stratosphere don't have any more time in a day or month than you do, so time management applied to goals is a powerful tool.

If you hit a single every time at bat, you will never lose.

As you might expect, the simplest methods are the best, none more so than the familiar Do List. Just list everything you have to do and then view these activities as small goals. Once the list is complete, review it again and prioritize the work, or goals, as A, B, or C items. "A" goals are those things that make you money today. "B" goals have the potential to become "A" goals if you run out of the latter. "C" goals stay put until they make the "B" list or are removed.

Using a Do List works because it makes your work relative by comparing some jobs to others. When going to work, tackle the most important goals first because they make the most difference. Work on the B goals next, then worry about the C group. More often than not, though, you will have created more A and B goals by then. That's a sign the system is working. When you complete any goal, mark it off the list. It may seem silly, but that's a reinforcing tactic—doesn't it feel great to look at a Do List with everything marked off? With each item you complete, you've hit another single.

The best time to create a Do List is at the end of the workday or work week. This is a good time-saving tactic, since you'll often forget over the weekend what was on your desk Friday afternoon. Consider this: It can take an hour to get restarted after a weekend. If you earn $100 per hour just once a week, it adds up to over $5,000 per year. The Do List thus becomes a memory device to maximize use of your time.

Your Do List can take shape in any form from a computer file to a cocktail napkin. Use the technique to capture all those wonderful ideas you have at odd times when you're thinking entrepreneurship. Put them in writing—all of them. I used to return from business trips with ideas written on all sorts of scraps of paper, which I gave to my executive secretary to decipher and turn into a list. That became my Do List, and you cannot imagine how many things I could complete as a result. Save the idea, put it on the list, then do it.

In the final analysis, setting goals is so important because one can't make a successful transition to entrepreneurship without them. It's a helpful process for all the reasons just described plus goals form the basis for writing business plans.

WRITE PLANS

There is never a shortage of investment money—only a shortage of investment plans. Written goals, in the form of a business plan, indicate the entrepreneur has carefully considered his or her ideas and intends to achieve them. Investors and potential associates will take these goals seriously, too, since the business plan is a road map and commitment to success. Entrepreneurs who do not plan cannot expect their ideas to be considered seriously. Try to get a business loan without one and you'll see what I mean.

Together with a partner I once planned the purchase of a fast food restaurant serving pizza and yogurt. That's an unusual but highly profitable combination. Because we didn't have any money, we prepared an extensive plan covering the acquisition and operational goals for one, three, and five years. A sellout price (reversion) at the end of the holding term was projected to estimate our overall total return on the investment. We wanted to borrow the acquisition price, my commission, and even the operating capital.

The first three bankers we talked to laughed us out of their banks. The fourth, a bank president, asked for a few days to study the proposal. Then he approved our loan, saying, "Anyone who has the ability to build a plan this good and the nerve to ask me to finance it has to be a good risk." Planning works.

Failing to plan while operating a business has consequences, one of which is frustration. Economic failure is another. For example, real estate agents fail to consider the reality of their career choice by failing to plan. They often start by imagining they will earn a 7 or 8 percent commission on annual sales of $1 million or more. That adds up (on just one million) to between $70,000 and $80,000 of earnings. Sounds great, but the dream fails to consider many things.

For example, 80 percent of real estate sales involve the participation of another agent who receives half the commission. The supervising agent's broker receives an average of one-third of the remaining share. An agent's expenses can easily be $500 per month. As a result of this breakdown, what looked like potential earnings of $70,000 per year is, in reality, $17,500. To actually achieve earnings of $70,000, the agent would need to sell over $4 million per year. Lack of such planning to prepare for this reality is one reason four of five real estate agents entering the business fail within five years. Similar statistics apply to start-up entrepreneurs.

A business plan is a written document describing the focus and type of activity your business will perform. It includes short- and long-term objectives (goals); a financial plan that forecasts income, expenses, and profit; and specific descriptions of strategies and tactics you'll use to cause the financial plan to occur.

Creating a business plan is an annual opportunity for management in any size company to push back away from the details of the day and review the big picture. It is a chance to check the direction and amount of progress being made, then adjust.

If it can't be written, it won't be done.

If you need further convincing, consider the following:

1. *Not writing your business plan is a cop-out.* Those who resist putting plans in writing may be painting themselves with the brush of inadequacy because they know they talk better than they do. In all but a few exceptions, people unwilling to write plans are also shaky on execution—they usually don't get results.

2. *Starting and building a business is a considerable challenge.* Writing the plan is the easy part. Creating a successful business involves executing a series of activities well enough to encourage people to pay for what you do. This takes patience, skill, focus, determination, and organization. A written business plan will give you all of these when you lose them temporarily.

3. *Maintaining a business on the road to growth is complex job.* There are too many things to do to

rely on memory alone. Your written plan breaks up the complexities into smaller parts that you can resolve a piece at a time. Then the work is easier to complete in the time you allot for it.

4. *The business plan is a benchmark to measure progress.* It quantifies performance in dollars and cents to illustrate where your business stands at the beginning of the year. In addition, monthly reviews of results allow you to compare actual events with the plan's forecast. This gives you a chance to take corrective action quickly if the business wanders off course.

5. *Business plans create accountability.* Entrepreneurs and employees alike must be accountable for results. There is no exception to this rule where a team goal is the objective—everyone must play his or her position. The results you see recorded and measured against expected performance are either favorable or not. If unfavorable, everyone pays the price with lower overall performance. If they're favorable, it's not an opportunity to relax. Here's a chance to dig in and "put some hay in the barn." Do less of what doesn't work and more of what does. Creating success is more exciting than having it. Written business plans can tell you how.

Writing a business plan is more time-consuming than difficult. The best way to make the exercise easier is to create or revise your plan the same time each year—well before it ends. Start with a vision of desired improvements and then work backwards, identifying what's needed to convert your vision into reality. Arrange the identified action steps in order of priority and attach a timetable. When complete, pull back and look at your overall strategy objectively. Does it make sense? Is it doable? Next, add financial results. Estimate, as accurately as possible, how much revenue your business will generate during the year. Break the sources of revenue down into different categories if possible, because some activities create more revenue than others. For example, convenience stores have fuel sales outside and grocery sales inside. Total volume can be several million dollars. Taken as a single indicator of performance, this seems impressive; however, fuel sales are often a large part of total volume, and they're not that profitable (5 percent or less). As a result, overall profit margins are not nearly as attractive as gross sales. It's important to know the source of sales and profit—then you know what deserves your attention.

When creating a revenue forecast, make logical premises to support your predictions. Write these up as notes you'll put in the back of the plan. Nothing is more embarrassing than sharing a forecast with a banker who wants to know how estimates were created and not having a logical answer. More important, the forecast is sure to be wrong. They almost always are. But having the forecast in writing provides an opportunity to refine your logic and improve. Without the plan, that's very difficult.

After creating an earnings estimate, start examining expenses. Group them into categories: Finance and Control, Marketing and Sales, Production and Service. Each area will have core strategies. To accomplish each strategy certain tactics will be necessary each day. Determine their cost, then add up the cost of all tactics. Add the cost of management strategies for each category. The combined total is your business overhead. Finally, subtract expenses from revenue. Is there a profit? Is it enough? Is there a loss? Adjust expenses to bring the profit in line with expectations while determining if a negative impact on sales will occur. In other words, would trimming certain tactics for expense reasons cause sales to fall off? Avoid changing (especially increasing) the revenue forecast. Maintain intellectual integrity. And remember that rule about percents—there are only one hundred of them. Making an adjustment in one area causes a change in others.

BE PREPARED *Nolo supre prendre* means "be prepared" to the entrepreneur. Latin for "no surprises," these words hang on my office wall now and have on many I've worked in over the years. Imagine how much more profitable business could be if there were no surprises. But that's an unrealistic wish. Goals and business plans force you to think things through and expect the unexpected. With minimal surprises, performance and profit are more likely to increase.

After setting goals and writing your plan, magnify its power by creating two additional versions. These can take shape in the form of amendments to Plan A and need not be so formal. Call them Plan B and Plan C.

Plan A describes what will happen if the business performs as expected. Plan B incorporates additional activity if results are better than you expected. Plan C covers how to respond if results are negative to plan. In each case, the financial component of the plan provides the yardstick to measure performance; the operations aspect of the plan is the "what to do, do more of, do less of" part.

Running a business in Plan A mode is easy since there are no surprises. Operating under Plan B or C is a more difficult (and frequent) reality. Plan B mode means results are occurring faster than anticipated. Rapidly growing businesses have difficulty because of the challenges associated with matching known expenses to an uncertain income forecast. This is a variable income operating with fixed expenses. For example, the cost of more production employees, inventory, and marketing tactics may need to increase to support the growth that's already underway. However, many of these costs are fixed and will not easily go away. Imagine the result of a decline in revenue after they're added. Timing is everything.

If unexpected growth accelerates beyond the pace predicted and expenses to support it are not increased accordingly, product quality, even availability, may suffer. Customer satisfaction could decline. Income may stall. To remove exposure to the downside of growth, successful entrepreneurs manage resources wisely and hold off increasing expenses for as long as possible. A good business plan helps you accurately predict the outcome of expanded investment, thereby reducing the exposure related to handling growth. As a result, you can grow at a pace that's manageable as well as affordable.

Plan C presents another type of challenge. Here revenue is declining but expenses are not. Profit is rapidly evaporating. There are only two ways to improve results: increase income and reduce expenses. A comprehensive business plan will help you find ways to consolidate or eliminate expenses altogether and assess the impact on profit. A word of caution, though. Reducing expenses is a temporary solution and a finite source of added revenue. To worsen the situation, your business's ability to perform may be unfavorably affected. Eventually reducing expenses can become a cycle that repeats itself until a company bleeds to death.

Increasing income is where to focus more attention when you're in Plan C mode. This is a difficult choice because it requires more creative approaches. Management thinking has to change. A growth wall may be present. Improvement by increasing income

Plan ahead ... it wasn't raining when Noah built the ark.

can, however, be infinite. Companies with substantial amounts of intellectual capital are more able to focus on increasing income that those with less.

The Entrepreneur's 12-Step Program acts as a comprehensive written business plan, enabling you to anticipate and prepare for whatever comes your way. When the unpredictable occurs, review the steps and select one that could apply. Put it to use. The program is a ratchet wrench to help manage your attitude and that of your business, too.

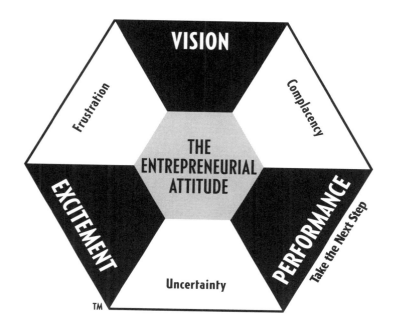

11. TAKE THE NEXT STEP

Have you ever heard someone say, "People teach or do, but not both?" This idea, which came up previously in Step 6, "Motivate with Leadership," is based on the notion that our differences become limitations. That seems like a pretty cruel and final verdict to deliver. Sometimes variances in priorities do, indeed, create differences among us, though.

Like time, business never stops.

Entrepreneurs teach themselves and then do what they've learned. If they don't, they fail. Next, they teach others to take on what they've been doing so they can go learn to do other things and grow. Thus, entrepreneurs apply teaching and doing to themselves first and foremost. The stimulus they need begins with the question, "What's the next step?" When they answer this, they act and advance.

My brokerage business, like most any business,

had an income cycle linked to a time span—in this case, about 90 to 120 days. During this time we would list, market, and sell properties. Knowing this taught me a good lesson: Today's paycheck is a result of what I did or didn't do about four months ago; therefore, the future is what I make of it today.

Seize the Here and Now

Make yourself this promise. Every day when you go to work, don't leave until you've done something that will advance your business—improve the chances it will make more money. It doesn't matter how long you stay on the job to get that done. Nor should you concern yourself (at first) with the size of consequences your actions will create. All that matters is your fulfillment of this commitment to make something happen every day. In time you'll learn what matters and what doesn't. Together these attributes will keep your business constantly advancing.

Entrepreneurs locate what they can do each day to improve business results by finding their worst problem and solving it, or taking a quick review of a Do List. Develop solutions; select the best one; then take action. Entrepreneurs who do this are never without something to do. They do not leave work until progress occurs.

Your business is always in motion because of your position relative to competitors. If they are advancing and you're not, you are heading backward. There is no standing still. As a result, successful entrepreneurs constantly search for the next step to take. Those who can take more of them, and faster, usually get bigger rewards. I called a nationally recognized entrepreneur once to see if he would sell a large tract of land to an investor I was representing. After introducing myself, he said one thing: "Shoot." This illustrates how a high-powered entrepreneur uses Step 11 of the Entrepreneur's 12-Step Program—he didn't mess around and got right to the point.

Entrepreneurs may come on strong like the one just described for two reasons. First, and obviously, they want to make as much happen as they can as fast as possible. Second, identifying people who take the next step and those who don't is important to entrepreneurs always searching for new contacts. They prefer to deal with those who do. This little bit of intimidation serves to determine whether you're serious and prepared to act by displaying your commitment to advance.

In a memorable movie called *The Shootist,* John Wayne plays a rough sheriff in the Old West who, at the end of his days, has established a considerable reputation for himself. Ron Howard, a young and impressionable admirer, asks the sheriff what's caused him to be so great. Wayne's reply went something like, "Well, it isn't because I'm so quick on the draw, because others are faster. And it's not because I can shoot so straight, because others are more accurate. I suppose it's because when it comes time to shoot, most men hesitate, just for a second, and I don't. I'm willing to pull the trigger." If you're tested and know what you're going to do next, don't be afraid to pull the trigger.

BE WILLING AND INFORMED

Unfortunately, you'll find intelligent business people everywhere who don't achieve the ranks of true leadership or legitimate success because they don't know what to do next. In many such cases they lack information, not ability.

Entrepreneurs normally do not need a kick in the pants to get going. In fact, just the opposite—they motivate themselves by constantly asking, "What's my next step here?" This serves to energize their search for answers, looking to their plan as well as asking for the opinion of others. This questioning state of mind is like a program running in the background alongside "think entrepreneurship"—it's called initiative.

Discipline helps put wheels on your initiative

and curiosity. It's a waste of time to create a solid business plan unless you intend to follow it. Equally fruitless is spending hours thinking through alternative options with the potential to improve business results and then cast them aside after a few minutes of resistance in the heat of action. Such an undisciplined approach can easily lead to failure. When entrepreneurs stick to the road map, their chances for success increase dramatically.

HELP OTHERS TAKE THEIR NEXT STEP

When leading others to improve results, you can create a performance-oriented atmosphere quickly with this step. When you establish yourself as a mover and shaker by taking the next step, there will be plenty of associates offering you an opportunity to take action for them, too. That's called putting their monkey on your back. When soliciting your opinion about a problem, they subtly attempt to convert your recommended solution to your responsibility for execution. Don't let it happen if you want to grow as an entrepreneur.

By all means listen to associates' problems. Then ask an inquiring co-worker what he or she thinks the next step to resolving it should be. It is amazing to see the blank look in response to such an obvious question. But sometimes it's exciting to see the look of illumination light up his or her face, too. And it is wonderful to see associates leave with their problem instead of leaving it with you. Others who answer your question quickly are showing early signs of leadership talent.

DEVELOP A SENSE OF URGENCY

A positive sense of urgency in the workplace is not characterized by a pressure-packed environment where everything must be done in a rush. Rather, it's a state of mind suggesting people have more fun being productive than at a standstill. A sense of urgency provides benefits for the entrepreneur, both intrinsic and extrinsic. You'll feel better, you'll improve efficiency, and you'll have more time for what really counts. It's as simple as that.

It's easier to get forgiveness than permission.

To maintain a healthy sense of urgency, successful entrepreneurs stay healthy themselves—that is, they eat right and exercise prudently. They understand good physical condition has a direct, favorable relationship to their performance. They keep their minds in shape, too, by cultivating a lifelong learning mode, characterized by a willingness to listen, read, and seek out relevant information. This helps them nurture an open mind and maintain a positive mental attitude, ready to act at all times. No negative waves.

When everyone else gives up, it's the entrepreneur who will find the energy and reason to continue. The only time you can lose is when you quit trying, and Step 11 of the Entrepreneur's 12-Step Program prevents that. Energy focused consistently on an objective propels entrepreneurs forward to defy the gravity of adversity, to launch and drive ideas until they reach escape velocity.

Working with a sense of urgency eventually starts to feed upon itself. Actions lead to more actions, with the motivator becoming the challenge of testing your limits, not just producing outcomes. When you reach this level of work ethic, performance expands. All of these things and more are possible when you constantly search, like a radar beacon, for the next step to take.

Successful behaviors lead into successful results.

The enemy of momentum is procrastination—the opposite of taking the next step and a behavior that will lead to failure. You will never see a truly successful entrepreneur act this way and you shouldn't either. Besides hurting yourself and your business, employees are very unfavorably affected by leaders who procrastinate. Not only will they feel frustrated and

PUT OFF PROCRASTINATION

demoralized; eventually they will follow your example or take a casual attitude toward work. Neither contributes to favorably to positive business results.

There are many reasons procrastination can get its foot in the door to your business. Entrepreneurship may be among the most rewarding, freedom-filled career choices available. But it's a tough job—as difficult and challenging as it is rewarding. You must be many things to many people, including yourself.

Charlie Podrebarac is a nationally syndicated cartoonist who produces the popular comic strips "Smart Alex" and "Cowtown." His talent also has been showcased in a book called *Night of the Living Bar-B-Q*. Charlie is an entrepreneur who works out of a studio in his home. Besides producing artwork he is his own janitor, secretary, bookkeeper, and doer of all the other jobs that go along with staying successful professionally. I'm sure Charlie would prefer to spend his time doing creative work, but he can't because hiring employees is not consistent with his idea of entrepreneurship. As a result, he does all the "dirty work," too. Procrastination would topple his balancing act very quickly.

As you make the transition to entrepreneurship by practicing the Entrepreneur's 12-Step Program, you must be willing to do everything it takes to succeed— when it needs to be done. Think carefully about all it will require to support your business idea. It's very possible you won't be able to afford help in the beginning; most entrepreneurs begin in a do-it-yourself profession. Don't let procrastination extort compromises and desperate shortcuts from you when you know your business deserves the cream of your efforts in a timely fashion.

Most people procrastinate out of fear of success, fear of failure, a "me-first" attitude, or just plain laziness. Whatever the reason, realize how very destructive this behavior can be.

In summary, there only two good things about pro-crastination: first, it offers a clear example of what you should not do if you want to make a successful transition to entrepreneurship, and second, if it exists you have a clear-cut opportunity for improvement!

Using a personal Do List each day is analogous to fol-lowing a business plan—it helps you find and take the next step. A good way to eliminate the pressure to per-form is knowing what you need to do next. Don't think (and fret); look at your list and act. Removing individ-ual activities from a Do List may not mean much; how-ever, the cumulative effect of removing 10 or 12 adds up to real progress. Forget about any job being too small to count; each represents forward movement and keeps the momentum alive.

WORK WITH PARTS, NOT THE SUM

Some goals are so big they encourage procrastina-tion. To avoid this paralysis, break your larger goals into smaller ones. An example of this happened in my franchise business. One of the more seasoned vice presidents was looking for ways to improve the per-formance of his sales force. He developed a good tech-nique to reduce big problems to little ones so they were less intimidating and easier to accomplish.

The formula was basic. First he clearly defined the goals for improved results that he wanted to achieve in his division. Next he determined what tactics on the part of his franchisees would contribute to the achievement of results he expected. Then he reduced these tactics to the most simple and easily under-stood value—a factor of one. For example, take one more listing; advertise one additional property, and so forth.

Finally, this remarkable VP taught his franchisees how to calculate the impact these small improve-ments could have on their business. He showed them the next step to put them to work. As a result of his "bite-size" approach, franchisees accepted his recommendations to improve individual and overall performance. Converting a business plan into a Do List of regular activity is empowering for entrepreneurs and all who work with them.

ATTACK! Another device entrepreneurs use to take the next step and encourage like performance from others is the "War Room"—a regularly scheduled meeting, sometimes held in a special location designated just for this purpose, where accountability is the rule of the day. In a war room, charts and graphs describing the performance of each key area of business activity are circulated to participants. Meetings are conducted to discuss the results achieved and look for next steps to improve. These are listed as goals and objectives.

Many people don't like a war room because it puts them on the spot. They may even make fun of it. But it can get results, building team spirit as well as establishing and maintaining a sense of urgency, too. Eventually the attitude has the potential to become a constructive device itself, encouraging progress at every step of the way.

You have to be willing to put one foot in front of the other—literally and figuratively—to make your transition to successful entrepreneurship. Ask yourself before beginning this path if you're willing, because if you aren't you can't. If that doesn't motivate you forward, then imagine continuing in conditions that will keep you anonymous until you retire. Ready to take that step?

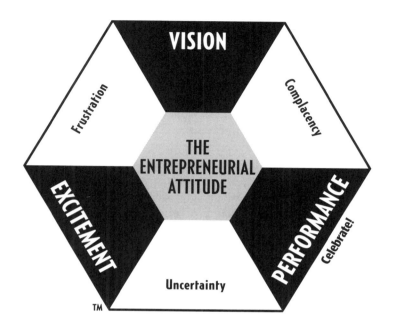

12. CELEBRATE!

This final step of the Entrepreneur's 12-Step Program may seem light-hearted, but it's truly just as important as the preceding 11. You must celebrate the good things that come your way. If you don't, your entrepreneurship is incomplete. Celebration sends out an unspoken but powerful invitation that you are willing to accept more.

As above, so below.

A higher power within the universe makes available an unlimited supply of unique energy—known by any name you wish to call it—to meet your limited demands. After tapping into it, your job is to focus this energy on your objectives, using your ability to recognize opportunity, build excitement to energize it, and perform the work to make it a reality. In so doing this universal energy is transformed and your goals appear.

> "Dream big dreams, think big thoughts, do big things. These are the things worth having."
> RAY WHEELER
> Arkansas
> Entrepreneur

Celebration is how you acknowledge the presence of this energy working for your benefit and signify your thanks with acceptance. This is a demonstration of humility, which is the strength to show you couldn't have accomplished what has been achieved by yourself. It indicates you are worthy and willing to receive the results created. More will come.

No one can tell you how to celebrate—that's for you to decide—but celebrate you must and on as many levels of consciousness as possible:

- Treat your spirit to an epiphany.
- Satisfy a curiosity of your mind.
- Explore your emotions with expressions of love, peace, and serenity.
- Excite your senses by doing something that makes you feel alive.

Leave nothing undone and no uncertainty about your acceptance of success by celebrating. When you internalize Step 12 of the Entrepreneur's 12-Step Program, your life and entrepreneurship become one continuous cycle of celebration; you make things happen you like; you accept them and start again. Mere survival disappears, replaced by your vision of opportunity and the power of your entrepreneurial attitude to grasp and share it with others.

In the end, the unmasking of an anonymous entrepreneur comes from ownership of a successful business that provides creative opportunities and supports a happy lifestyle. Entrepreneurship can elicit what you desire from a career. Fulfillment and security grow from the uniqueness you express. The inevitable profit and wealth created make it possible for you to afford a luxurious assortment of choices. Go ahead—celebrate!

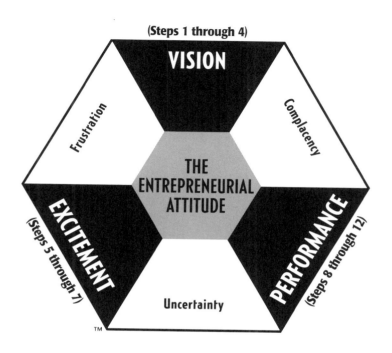

NEW ENDINGS COME FROM NEW BEGINNINGS.

CHAPTER FIVE

ENTREPRENEURS: ENGINES OF FREE ENTERPRISE

Entrepreneurship is business ownership. Business ownership creates profit. Profit creates wealth. Wealth creates freedom and lifestyle choices. This pursuit has beckoned creative risk takers since the Phoenicians first sailed on trade missions out of the Mediterranean nearly 5,000 years ago. It is an integral part of the spirit that built America. Statesmen like Benjamin Franklin were entrepreneurs, and pioneers like Lewis and Clark and Davey Crockett were, too. America offered them opportunity. It always has and still provides new arrivals with a safe harbor of political freedom and the hope to build financial autonomy. The concept will endure and spread as entrepreneurship finds more ports of call worldwide.

The desire to become a successful entrepreneur is strong. The risk of loss is not always a deterrent. Consider these statistics from *The State of Small Business: A Report of the President, 1995*: "Most firms fail during their early years. For a given cohort, about 20 percent of the remaining firms fail in each of the first and second years after startup. The rate of failure decreases year-by-year; by the ninth or tenth year only about 7 or 8 percent of the cohort remainder fail. Fewer than half of all new firms are in operation after five years."

WHY ENTREPRENEURSHIP?

Despite the high risk of entrepreneurship indicated by these data, many that attempt entrepreneurship, and fail, will not abandon their goal of entrepreneurial success. Risk does not drive people away from this career option. *The Function of Failure,* a research report completed by M & R Associates, Richard F. Fullenbaum and Mariana A. McNeill, concludes the following: "The responses [of their survey group] to two speculative questions capture important non-economic aspects of the bankruptcy experience. When asked 'If you were to do it all over again, would you have started your bankrupt business?' 61.4% of the respondents answered 'Yes.' When asked 'Would you ever start your own business again?' 73.2 percent answered 'Yes.'" Obviously entrepreneurship is no passing fancy, easily dismissed—it's here to stay.

Small business is the vehicle driving entrepreneurship, and nearly all entrepreneurs start out small. They begin with very little money, acquire a franchise, or leverage their way into an existing business. In fact, the role of small business entrepreneurs in the U.S. is very significant. Information provided by the United States SBA Office of Advocacy shows small businesses 1) provided virtually all new jobs from 1991 to 1995; 2) were 99.7 percent of all employers in 1993; 3) employed 53 percent of the private workforce in 1993; 4) provided 47 percent of receipts (sales) in 1993; 5) provided 55 percent of all innovations according to a 1982 survey; 6) accounted for 31 percent of all direct and indirect federal contract dollars for 1993; 7) were accountable for 25 percent of the jobs in high technology sectors in 1991; and 8) accounted for 50 percent of the private sector input in 1982.

These are impressive statistics. Clearly, the family farm that provided financial autonomy decades ago has evolved into the small business of today and the next millenium.

EXPANSION PLANS Global networking creates entrepreneurial opportunity at levels not previously available to the small business entrepreneur. Anyone can acquire access to a worldwide marketplace for a small investment in a computer with communication linkages. The popularity of this path in America is well documented in *The State of Small Business: A Report of the President, 1995,* which states that in addition to 22 million small businesses already in existence, "a record 807,000 new small firms with employees were added in that same year—a 2.4 percent increase. The number of these firms has increased fairly steadily over the past decade, and in 1993 and 1994 successive new highs for this measure were established."

Starting is the hardest part of anything.

Clearly, the idea of entrepreneurship is growing, and America provides an example that many in other countries want to follow. Hundreds of millions of people worldwide want to try entrepreneurship. In China, India, Indonesia, Europe, South America, Australia, and elsewhere, budding entrepreneurs are embracing the dream of financial freedom and security offered by exploring their business ideas with increasingly cooperative political environments.

Women are among the fastest growing groups of entrepreneurs. According to research conducted by the United States Small Business Administration:

- In the past 10 years the number of self-employed women has increased at six times the rate of men.
- Women business owners are starting businesses at twice the rate of their male counterparts.
- Projections estimate women will own 40 percent of all businesses by the year 2000.
- Women employ 11 million workers, more than the Fortune 500 companies worldwide. (Source: National Foundation for Women Business Owners)

Changing trends suggest entrepreneurship is increasingly linked to the desire for lifestyle changes. Rapid-fire information-sharing capabilities in entrepreneurship are fueling a surge in the number of home-based business owners and telecommuters. These are horizon careers.

According to *The Annual Report on Small Businesses and Competition* prepared for *The State of*

Small Business: A Report of the President, 1995,"Working out of the home has become a significant and growing phenomenon in the United States. There are two types of home-based workers: 'home-based business owners,' who are self-employed individuals operating a business or profession primarily from or in a home office; and 'telecommuters'—employees who do office work at home during normal business hours." The report continues, "The May 1991 Current Population Survey identified 5.6 million primary home-based businesses and 1.9 million telecommuters. Nearly 7.5 million home-based entrepreneurs altogether." And further, "Owning a home-based business and working at home for wages are both labor market options that offer flexibility to entrepreneurs and employees."

President Bill Clinton, as quoted in the June 19, 1997, issue of *The Wall Street Journal,* said home-based businesses are expanding even more rapidly. The article said the President favored expanding the tax deduction for people who work out of their homes. He said there were three million such people when he was elected in 1992, that the number has ballooned to 12 million today, and it's headed to 30 million.

Many would rather invest in a first class entrepreneur with a second class concept than a first class concept with a second class entrepreneur.

The principles of entrepreneurship are taught throughout life, beginning early. How many lemonade stands set up in your neighborhood over the average summer? Kids are also encouraged more formally to consider a profession of business ownership by private and public foundations who create and offer entrepreneurial programs. Project HOPE+E, based in Wichita, Kansas, is a program designed to teach the basics of business ownership to fifth-grade students. The Kauffman Foundation in Kansas City, Missouri (one of the largest in the nation), identifies children as targets for entrepreneurial education, too. The Rothman Institute of Entrepreneurial Studies at

Fairleigh Dickinson University, in a report titled *Entrepreneurship as a Career Path,* suggests more students would prefer to have their own business. In addition, the report indicates 7 of 10 high school students want to start a business one day, and 4 of 5 students believe it is very important to teach more entrepreneurship in high school and college. Further, hundreds of U.S. colleges offer academic courses and programs on entrepreneurship. Everywhere you look the seeds of business ownership are falling on fertile soil.

Whether you realize it not, we all participate in entrepreneurship by being one ourselves or working for someone else who is. Since the United States SBA estimates one-third of all Americans are thinking of owning their own business at any time, at least 91 million people would like to trade places.

COMMON PEOPLE DOING UNCOMMON THINGS

Regardless of global geography, Main Street is the proving ground and launch pad of entrepreneurs. No business makes it to Wall Street without running this gauntlet first. The challenges are direct, personal, and feel like the whole world is watching. This is where you find the real entrepreneurs attempting to replace survival in an unfulfilling job or business with the celebration of success.

The mainstream of entrepreneurs own successful local businesses. They include the grocer, dentist, accountant, dry cleaner, jeweler, frozen yogurt shop owner, or fast-food franchisee, and all the other small-business people you deal with daily. These are the "do-it-yourself" entrepreneurs that make the world go round—the engines of free enterprise.

QUALITIES OF AN ENTREPRENEUR

1. **ENERGETIC:** Entrepreneurs are people who stay healthy, eat right, and exercise. They know energy is a valuable resource in making things happen.

2. **DRIVEN:** Entrepreneurs' motivation is fueled by self-confidence, high self-esteem, a positive mental attitude, and avoidance of negative people. They have a life-long learning mode, characterized by a willingness to listen, read, and seek information.

3. **LONG-TERM PLAYER:** Entrepreneurs are not motivated by "get rich quick" schemes. They do not implement short-term thinking at the expense of long-term results. As a result they stay out of crisis management.

4. **MONEY ISN'T EVERYTHING:** Entrepreneurs know money is but one measure of success. They see the value of balance and success on all the playing fields of life.

5. **PERSISTENT:** Entrepreneurs are problem solvers. They know the absence of a problem is the biggest problem — someone is in the kitchen playing with matches. They enjoy fixing things and require constant challenges, or they lose interest.

6. **GOAL ORIENTED:** Entrepreneurs have vision. Experience has usually taught them the value of defined objectives to help them maintain a clear sense of direction.

7. **RISK ORIENTED:** Entrepreneurs aren't afraid to take risk because they perform better under pressure. Their desire to maintain a base of security, however, moderates the amount of risk they are willing to accept.

8. **DYNAMIC:** Entrepreneurs can deal with failure because they know it's the other side of the coin of success. Failure is not fatal, and it's not final. These people understand failure as an opportunity — an improved chance to succeed — because they have removed one more thing that can go wrong.

9. **SELF-STARTER:** Entrepreneurs take the initiative and seek personal responsibility. These people are "do-it-yourselfers" and don't need permission to act. They know they can rise to any occasion by taking control of themselves first.

10. **HIGH STANDARDS:** Entrepreneurs compete against self-imposed standards. No one knows their limits better than themselves. And their standards will usually exceed those set by others.

QUALITIES OF AN ENTREPRENEUR (CONT.)

10. HIGH STANDARDS: Entrepreneurs compete against self-imposed standards. No one knows their limits better than themselves. And their standards will usually exceed those set by others.

11. COMFORTABLE WITH CHAOS: Entrepreneurs have a high tolerance for ambiguity or uncertainty. It is possible for entrepreneurs to manage multiple projects in various stages of development. They will quickly "do what works" rather than follow the rules if they don't apply.

12. NEXUS: Entrepreneurs become the brain trust of a business by linking themselves to all aspects of the operation. From this seat of influence they manage information like it's money.

CHAPTER SIX

LIVING WELL IS THE BEST PROFIT

Entrepreneurship for the money certainly is exciting, but eventually that focus becomes a hollow victory. Remember, finding outlets for creative expression provide the greatest fulfillment to most people—financial compensation is extra. So it is with the Entrepreneur's 12-Step Program.

Use this program to erase uncertainty, complacency, and frustration by building new awareness. Construct an entrepreneurial attitude and it becomes nothing less than a sturdy platform to support a new life. Frontiers open as old limitations fade. Recognition, excitement, and performance are the by-products of this new state of mind. All areas of your life in addition to your career improve, so living well becomes the best profit of all.

Your transition to entrepreneurship will not occur overnight. The attitude that keeps you anonymous may have been around for years and bad habits die hard. But progress is a functional reality you can achieve. Focus on learning to manage that old attitude with new, more powerful behaviors such as those described in the Entrepreneur's 12-Step Program. Then, without any influence, it makes no difference if old ideas stick around or not.

The mechanisms to practice these steps and responsible entrepreneurship surround you. Looking into the next century we see even more opportunity as greater emphasis is placed on the individual's power to achieve financial autonomy and desire for creative fulfillment. Entrepreneurship invites direct participation beginning with you, the seed corn for a record harvest of entrepreneurs leaving the survival mentality for a celebration of success.

BIBLIOGRAPHY AND RECOMMENDED READING

Bond, Robert E., Susan Moulton, and Jeff Bond. *Bond's Franchise Guide: 1996 Edition.* Oakland, CA: SourceBook Publications, 1996.

Chamberlain, Roscoe L. *The United Way: A Manual of Helpful Suggestions.* Kansas City, MO: United Farm Agency, 1965.

DePree, Max. *Leadership Is an Art.* New York: Bantam Doubleday Dell, 1989.

Entrepreneurship as a Career Path. Rutherford, NJ: Rothman Institute of Entrepreneurial Studies, Fairleigh Dickinson University, n.d.

Farson, Richard. *Management of the Absurd: Paradoxes in Leadership.* New York: Simon & Schuster, 1996.

Fezler, William. *Total Visualization Using All Five Senses.* New York: Simon & Schuster, 1989.

Fritz, Robert. *The Path of Least Resistance: Principles for Creating What You Want to Create.* Walpole, NH: Stillpoint Publishing, 1987.

Fullenbaum, Richard F., and Mariana A. McNeill. *The Function of Failure.* Springfield, VA: National Information Technical Service, U.S. Department of Commerce, 1994.

Geneen, Harold, with Alvin Moscow. *Managing.* New York: Avon Books, 1985.

Gibran, Kahlil. *The Prophet.* New York: Alfred A. Knopf, 1973.

Hall, Robert E., and Alvin Rabushka. *The Flat Tax.* Stanford, CA: Hoover Institution Press, 1995.

Hawken, Paul. *Growing a Business.* New York: Simon & Schuster, 1987.

Heider, John. *The Tao of Leadership: Leadership Strategies for a New Age.* New York: Bantam Books, 1985.

Johnson, Robert A. *Owning Your Own Shadow: Understanding the Dark Side of the Psyche.* HarperCollins, 1991.

————. *She: Understanding Feminine Psychology.* Revised Edition. New York: Harper & Row, 1989.

Keyes, Ken Jr. *The Hundredth Monkey.* St. Mary, KY: Vision Books, 1981.

Levinson, Jay Conrad. *Guerrilla Marketing: Secrets for Making Big Profits from Your Small Business.* Boston: Houghton Mifflin, 1984.

Lidell, Lucy Narayani, and Giris Rabinovitch. *The Sivananda Companion to Yoga: A Complete Guide to Physical Postures, Breathing Exercises, Diet, Relaxation and Meditation Techniques of Yoga.* New York: Simon & Schuster, 1983.

Mackay, Harvey. *Swim with the Sharks without Being Eaten Alive: Outsell, Outmarket, Outmotivate, and Outnegotiate Your Competition.* New York: William Morrow, 1988.

Mok, Paul P. *Survey of Communicating Styles.* Plano, TX: Training Associates Press, n.d. (Available from P.O. Box 940970, Plano, TX 75094; 800-779-3536)

Molton, Warren Lane. *Friends, Partners, & Lovers: Marks of a Vital Marriage.* Valley Forge, PA: Judson Press, 1993.

One Day at a Time in Al-Anon. New York: Al-Anon Family Group Headquarters, 1988.

Osborne, Richard L. "Second Phase Entrepreneurship: Breaking through the Growth Wall." *Business Horizons,* January-February, 1994.

Peter, Laurence J., and Raymond Hull. *The Peter Principle: Why Things Always Go Wrong.* New York: Bantam Books, 1970.

Popkin, Joel, and Company. *Business Survival Rates by Age Cohort of Business.* Springfield, VA: National Information Technical Service, U.S. Department of Commerce, n.d.

Pratte, Joanne H. *Myths and Realities of Working at Home: Characteristics of Homebased Business Owners and Telecommuters.* Springfield, VA: National Information Technical Service, U.S. Department of Commerce, n.d.

Price, John Randolph. *The Superbeings: Overcoming Limitations through the Power of the Mind.* Carlsbad, CA: Hay House Publishers, 1997.

Raffe, Sydelle, Eric Sloan, and Mary Vencill. *How Small Businesses Learn.* Springfield, VA: National Information Technical Service, U.S. Department of Commerce, 1994.

Sagan, Carl. *The Dragons of Eden: Speculations on the Evolution of Human Intelligence.* New York: Random House, 1977.

Schwartz, David J. *The Magic of Thinking Big.* New York: Simon & Schuster, 1982.

Simmons, Chad. *Rule of Thumb: The Standard in Pricing Small*

Business. Kansas City, MO: Corinth Press, 1991.

Speller, Jon P. *Seed Money in Action.* New York: Morning Star Press, 1965.

The State of Small Business: A Report of the President, 1995. Washington, DC: U.S. Government Printing Office, 1996.

Walton, Mary. *The Deming Management Method.* New York: Perigree Books, 1986.

Wycoff, Joyce. *Mindmapping: Your Personal Guide to Exploring Creativity and Problem Solving.* New York: Berkley Books, 1991.

INDEX

small business owners, 1, 2, 17, 97, 98, 158
stock market, 108-109
strengths and weaknesses, types of, 55
supply and demand, 126, 134
synergy, 25, 86

T

target market, 102, 124, 125, 126-128
tax code, 53-54
teaching/training, 83-84, 145
teamwork, 58, 79-80, 85-86, 122
telecommuters, 2, 159-160
time management, 136-137, 146, 151, 152
TQM (Total Quality Management), 6

U

uniqueness, fostering, 17

United States Small Business Administration, 2, 158, 159, 161
urgency, role of, 148-149

V

values, core business, 14, 15, 16-17, 113-114
vision, 4, 7, 11, 15, 22, 36, 45, 51, 57, 64, 65, 87, 140; inspiring with, 69; power of, 70-71; shaping a, 73-75; sharing a, 75-78; sources of, 72-73

W

war room, creating a, 152
waste elimination, 120-122
web-type organizations, 5-6

PERSONAL NOTES